Cultu
& Spo

HENRY COOPER

NORMAN GILLER

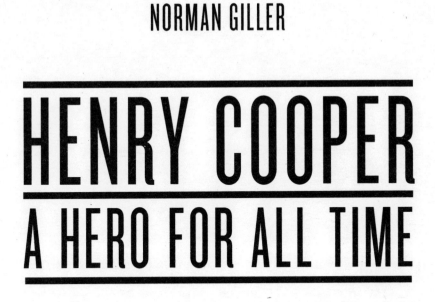

HENRY COOPER
A HERO FOR ALL TIME

The Robson Press

First published in Great Britain in 2012 by
The Robson Press (an imprint of Biteback Publishing Ltd)
Westminster Tower
3 Albert Embankment
London
SE1 7SP

ISBN 978-1-84954-159-6

In loving memory
of Sir Henry
and Lady Albina Cooper

ACKNOWLEDGEMENTS

The author thanks the premier photographic agency, the Press Association, for the majority of the photographs and Jane Speed for her research assistance. Thanks also to the Cooper family, Terry Baker of A1 Sporting Speakers, to Roy Ullyett's estate and, in particular, to freelance artist Art Turner for his sketches. Norman Giller also wishes to place on record his appreciation for the enthusiasm and skill of Jeremy Robson and his publishing team, with special mention for Helen Zaltzman, designer Namkwan Cho and master editor Sam Carter.

CONTENTS

FOREWORD
JIMMY GREAVES

Henry Cooper was a treasured pal of mine for more than fifty years and he rates up there with Bobby Charlton as the greatest of all British sporting heroes. Wherever you go in the world, everybody knows Bobby and Our Enery.

Sir Bobby found fame with his feet, Sir Henry with his fists. Bobby had his bombshell shot, Enery his 'ammer. Both represented their sport and their country with a dignity and sportsmanship that should be bottle-fed to many of today's overpaid, pampered stars, who seem to think sporting celebrity gives them the right to become men behaving badly. There was never a time when our two favourite sporting knights had to reach for the protection of a court injunction.

There were several of us at Spurs who were boxing fans and we used to watch him in his major contests. When he knocked down Cassius Clay at Wembley Stadium in 1963, I willed the man who was to become Muhammad Ali to stay down, but the bell saved him.

Henry and I started out together as professional sportsmen round about the same time, he as a boxer in South London and I as a footballer with Chelsea in West London. Our paths often crossed at various sporting dinners and charity events, and I always found him great company, ever ready to share the latest joke and a laugh. In recent years I got to know Henry even better because we travelled together to appear in the road shows organised by our chum Terry Baker, of AI Sporting Speakers.

I have known Norman Giller for even longer than I knew Henry. He first interviewed me for the local West Ham newspaper where he worked when we were both seventeen, and I have been trying to avoid him ever since. Twenty books together later, I guess I have been unable to shake him off.

I last saw Norman and Henry together at the funeral of Norman's lovely wife, Eileen. She and Norman were married for forty-five years. Henry and Albina had an idyllic marriage that matched theirs and when I heard Albina had died, I feared for Aitch. She was his right and left hand, and I worried how he was going to cope without her. Shortly after came the news that his identical twin brother George had passed on and the last time I saw Henry at a road show I knew he was in trouble. He had lost his old spirit and sparkle, and I was not surprised when he took the final count.

But let's remember the Henry Cooper who was loved by millions and gave loads of pleasure with his boxing performances and, later, his easy-going nature and willingness to help anybody in dire straits. The staggering amount of time he gave to charity was never for show but out of deep sincerity.

His life and times are well chronicled here by a writer who knew him better than most. We will definitely not see his like again. Rest easy, Aitch.

HENRY COOPER: A HERO FOR ALL TIME

INTRODUCTION
HENRY MARCO COOPER AND JOHN PIETRO COOPER

Our Dad became a household name as Henry Cooper, a champion boxer of renown and much admired beyond the boundaries of sport by many people captured by his natural desire to give more than he took from life. We are enormously proud of all that he achieved, not only in the boxing ring, but outside with his many unselfish acts and services to charities that, to his immense pride, earned him a knighthood. Dad did not seek reward for his charity work. He saw it as a duty, having come from a humble background, and never lost sight of the fact that there were those in need who required help, support and funding.

It was distressing to lose Dad on May Day 2011, his passing coming quickly in the wake of losing his best friend, our Mum, Albina, and his beloved identical twin brother George. For we 'boys', it was a triple blow from which we have yet to recover, but the warmth of our memories of three greatly loved people is gradually replacing the pain of the loss.

Eventually, we intend to produce our own special memorial tribute to our dad and mum. In the meantime, we are very happy to give our blessing to this highly personal book by author Norman Giller. He was there as a witness almost from the start of Dad's boxing career and their boxer/reporter relationship blossomed into a friendship that later encompassed our mum and Norman's late wife, Eileen.

There is much new material in this book that not even we knew about Dad's life and career, and we see it as a fitting homage not only to Henry Cooper the boxer but also to Henry Cooper, our dad, our Hero.

Author Norman Giller is making a donation to the Sir Henry Cooper Charity Fund in memory of his old friend, and as a gesture for the support he has received from Henry's sons in the writing of this tribute memoir.

SECONDS OUT
NORMAN GILLER

This was planned as an autobiography and Henry's first words were going to be: 'It's been quite a life so far, and I want to get some memories down on paper before the final bell…'

Sadly, we never got round to writing what would have been Sir Henry's own intimate account of his life and times. The final bell rang earlier and more suddenly than any of us expected.

The great man's demise came quickly after the double blow of losing his beloved wife, Albina, and identical twin brother, George, within a short period of time. Our mutual mate, Colin Hart, the doyen of boxing scribes, summed it up when he said: 'Henry died of a broken heart.'

How tragically ironic for a man who was all heart.

The day Henry died – May Day 2011 – Britain lost a national treasure. His fame and popularity transcended the world of boxing in which he made an international name for himself as a heavyweight boxing champion, fighting with skill, power and the quiet dignity that marked just about everything he did in life. Oh yes, and he famously knocked down one Cassius Marcellus Clay – much more of that later.

I had known and loved – yes, loved – 'Our Enery' for more than fifty years and I have been encouraged to go ahead with this book by Henry's devoted sons, Henry Marco and John Pietro, as a personal memoir of a man among men and one of the most agreeable people ever to cross my path during this ephemeral existence of ours.

It had been planned as the fourth book I had written with Henry, following on from *Henry Cooper's 100 Greatest Boxers*, *Henry Cooper's Most Memorable Fights* and *Henry Cooper's How to Box*.

I approached entrepreneur Terry Baker, a friend and near neighbour of mine in Dorset, who promoted Henry's popular road show appearances, about the feasibility of publishing a limited edition autobiography, each copy signed by Henry. What a collector's item that would have been!

We were about to discuss it with Henry Marco in his role as his dad's business manager when alarm bells started ringing about our hero's health. It seemed almost overnight he went from the affable, happy Henry we all knew and adored to a shuffling shadow.

In a matter of months he had passed on, leaving behind a mournful army of admirers whose lives he had brightened with his pleasing personality and presence, as well as with his achievements.

In his warm eulogy at Henry's moving private funeral in Tonbridge, Kent, comedian Jimmy Tarbuck said: 'Henry was a nice man... a very nice man.' That captured Henry, simply but perfectly. Yes, a *very* nice man.

The publishing baton was picked up by Jeremy Robson, renowned for his illustrious sports publishing ventures over more than forty years. He agreed with me that Henry deserved a biography, putting in context not only his exceptional boxing performances but also his impact as a hero of the people, going far beyond the world of sport.

In the following pages I plan to paint a personal portrait of Sir Henry that I hope is both accurate and worthy of a man who won the hearts of the nation, with both his fistic feats and his exhaustive work for charities that was appropriately rewarded with a widely welcomed knighthood.

The quotations I use throughout the book were gathered over years and from scores of conversations with Henry, and I hope his voice comes through to give meat and merit to my memories. Nobody can paint a portrait of our hero without dipping into the meticulous autobiography produced in partnership with former *Guardian* sports editor John Samuel (Cassell, 1974) or the more cerebral biography from Robert Edwards (BBC Worldwide).

Oliver Cromwell instructed his portrait artist Sir Peter Lely: 'Paint me warts an' all.' Well, I have spoken to scores of people who knew Henry inside and outside the ring, and I cannot come up with a single blemish. Mind you, his old nemesis Brian London confided: 'He could be as nice as pie one minute and then knock ten skittles out of you the next...' I've cleaned that up.

But that was Henry's brutal business and he went about it in an assassin's thoroughly professional manner, yet somehow managing to retain his self-respect at all times, even when he was on the receiving end of the punches and the punishment.

One skeleton in his closet: he was an Arsenal fan. But nobody's perfect (this written as somebody with Tottenham leanings, always a subject for rivalry and banter between us). You judge a sporting hero not only on how he performs in the sports arena, but also his behaviour away from the cheering throng. Can he meet Rudyard Kipling's twin impostors of triumph and disaster and treat them both the same?

Henry had a quiet grumble about a few of the results that went against him, particularly in his farewell fight against Joe Bugner. But outside the ring his general behaviour was impeccable and an example to today's high-profile sportsmen and women as to how to conduct themselves in public and in private.

Yes, Henry Cooper – Our Enery – was a hero for all time.

Come with me now to the springtime of his life as I tell the Henry Cooper story over fifteen rounds, which fittingly was the championship distance when he was hitting and hurting for a living.

Seconds out, here comes Our Enery...

THE BISHOP AND THE TWINS

Our first meeting: it was 5.15 a.m. on a freezing December morning in 1958 and Henry Cooper was standing alongside me stark naked, apart from a pair of heavy-duty size eleven army boots.

No, I am not uncovering a sordid kinky secret from Henry's past. I had asked for an interview for a feature I was writing for the fight game trade paper *Boxing News* and Cooper's manager Jim Wicks told me in raw, unadulterated Cockney: 'The only time that he's got to rabbit to you, my son, is when he goes on his early morning gallop. So get a pair of strong daisies and join him on the old frog if you want any nannies.'

Meet The Bishop – Jim Wicks, the most influential and important man in Henry's life and boxing career. Jim was not just his manager, he was his minder, mentor and best mate. And an unknowing master of malapropisms.

Very misleadingly, he was called 'The Bishop' because of his distinguished, benign looks and bald dome that would have fitted perfectly into a mitre. But ex-bookmaker Jim's church was the betting shop and his altar rails were at the racecourse. In those pre-mobile days he would eat only at restaurants where there was a portable payphone that could be brought to the table, so that he was able to place bets throughout the meal. Win or lose, his poker face gave nothing away and his mood would never change from amiable, and he always picked up the bill.

Jim and his betting cronies could have stepped out of the Cockney equivalent of Damon Runyon's *Guys and Dolls*, a sort of *Geezers and Birds*. I wish I had the Runyonesque skill to transfer them to the page, the likes of ticket spivs and gamblers synonymous: Johnny the Stick, One-Arm Lou, Fat Stan, Razor Laugh, The Hat, Italian Al, Beryl the Peril (the first female boxing promoter, Beryl Gibbons), Harry the Hoarse and, of course, The Bishop. Come to think of it, scriptwriter John Sullivan managed it with *Only Fools and Horses*.

These were the sort of Del Boy oddballs surrounding Henry. But he never allowed himself to become distracted, tainted or stained by them, just nicely amused by the sort of larger-than-life Cockney characters you just don't see around anymore. Jim Wicks, ex-publican son of a Bermondsey docker and a pioneer of sporting spin and propaganda, was the most memorable of them all.

I will translate for The Bishop as we go along. 'A pair of strong daisies' – daisy roots, boots. 'Frog' – frog and toad, road. 'Nannies' – nanny goats, quotes.

Our meeting place for the early morning road run was the Thomas a Becket gymnasium, bang in Del Boy territory down the Old Kent Road, where Henry was training for an upcoming challenge for the British and Empire heavyweight titles against his old foe Brian London at Earls Court.

He ran a regular four miles around South London streets every morning before they became polluted by traffic fumes and here I was about to accompany him, along with his spitting-image twin brother

George and trainer Danny Holland, who allowed himself the luxury of a bicycle. I introduced myself to Henry and he showed no embarrassment as he warmly shook my hand while wearing nothing but his boots.

'Watchyer, Norm,' he said with his huge trademark smile, instantly putting me at my ease as if we were old mates. 'I always put me boots on first. It's habit from when I'm getting ready to fight – boots first, then jockstrap, protector, shorts, hand bandages and me dressing gown last. Then the gloves of course, yeah.'

He had a rhythmic way of talking that you could have set to a snare drum accompaniment and he would invariably end a staccato run of sentences with a sign-off 'yeah', like a cymbal crash from a percussionist. Sometimes, as if influenced by the Beatles, he would put in a 'yeah, yeah, yeah'. It was the equivalent of Frank Bruno's 'Know wot I mean?' or the 'y'know' of a million Cockneys, a spoken punctuation mark.

Henry pointed down at the boots. 'These are all I've got to show for serving Queen and Country.'

'King and country, 'n' all,' chipped in brother George, who was already in his Army boots and tracksuit. 'We swore allegiance to King George when we started our National Service and the Queen was on the throne by the time we were demobbed.'

If you had your back to the Cooper twins you had no idea which one was talking because their voices were of the same timbre and tone, and for such big men surprisingly soprano-pitched at times, particularly when they were excited.

I had just stripped off and was about to pull on a tracksuit when The Bishop arrived, looking immaculate as if he were on his way to morning prayers. A smart, grey trilby protected his bald head from the cold morning air and he was sheathed in a fine-check Crombie overcoat. He had probably just come from a Mayfair casino or an all-night card school.

'Bleedin' 'ell,' he said, catching sight of my skinny-as-a-pipe-cleaner, nine stone featherweight frame alongside the, by comparison, perfectly chiselled Adonis that was Our Enery. I was a blushing boy of nineteen, Henry at his physical peak of twenty-five. 'I've got greyhounds fatter than you,' said Jim, in unmerciful mood. 'You need a good meal rather than a good run. For gawd's sake, Enery, don't let him fall down any drains.'

Henry came to my defence. 'Don't listen to him, Norm,' he said. 'You can't fatten thoroughbreds.'

From that day on it was a catchphrase between the two of us, as what started out as a working relationship blossomed over the next fifty-plus years into strong friendship.

Four weeks later Henry took the British and Empire titles away from Brian London with a convincing fifteen rounds points victory. I told him that it was down to the fast pace I had set in our road run together. It was not at all funny but Henry, bless him, was polite enough to laugh. 'Yeah, Norm, yeah,' he said. That somehow captured his spirit of generosity.

★ ★ ★

Henry and George had been born in the York Road hospital, Westminster, on 3 May 1934. George V was on the throne, Ramsay MacDonald was leading a coalition government, Hitler was about to declare himself Führer, the Ambling Alp Primo Carnera was world heavyweight champion, Agatha Christie wrote *Murder on the Orient Express*, a pint of beer cost twopence and a semi-detached house in London would set you back £800, and more than 40 per cent of people in the United Kingdom – including the Coopers – were living on or below the poverty line.

Henry arrived twenty minutes before his brother and weighed in at 6lb 4oz, two pounds lighter than George, who remained slightly heavier throughout their lives. As they grew up, the only way that people – other than their mum and dad and older brother Bernard – could tell them apart was that George was right-handed, Henry left-handed. They were mirror twins. There were times when even their father, Henry Senior – himself once a handy fighter – got muddled up and paddled the arse of Henry Junior for something George had done, or vice versa.

It came as quite a shock to Mum when we were born because she was expecting one baby and she was going to call us Walter. A nurse looked at us and said, 'They seem like a right Henry and George to me.' So that's what we became rather than Walter.

Our first home was at Camberwell Green, which adjoins Lambeth, but we always think of ourselves as Bellingham boys from Lewisham in South-East London. We grew up on the council estate there and it was at Bellingham Boxing Club where we first started taking the old fight game seriously. We were what was called, back in those days, ruffians, but we respected our teachers and lived in fear of Dad's slaps if we back-chatted him or failed to do whatever Mum wanted. Dad used the same discipline on us as his dad used on him. Granddad George was a notorious cobbles fighter, who used to scrap for pennies round the Elephant and Castle area, and Dad would cop a right hander from him if he misbehaved. In our time it was all right to whack your kids and teachers would cane you or slap your arse with a slipper. Somewhere between the way they disciplined us then and the namby-pamby way they treat children today would be about right. You have to teach them respect. My boys, Henry Marco and John Pietro, have had quite a few hand whacks on the bum when they've got up to mischief. Nothing heavy, but enough to show them the difference between right and wrong.

George and me grew up when there were a lot of villains around, blokes who would use violence to get what they wanted. But that was never our game. The only real naughties we got up to was nicking balls from the local golf course, mostly from the lake, and then we'd sell them to club members for half-a-crown. Golf was then a rich man's sport. Little did I know that it would become my passion, slicing plenty of balls into lakes but with no urchins to sell them back to me for half a dollar.

We had loads of energy to burn, and boxing proved the ideal outlet and kept us on the straight and narrow. I suppose we might have run with the hounds but for boxing. We grew up in the Teddy Boy days when there used to be gang fights, with knuckledusters, bicycle chains, razors and flick knives. But me and George kept out of all that, thanks to boxing. Anyhow, neither of us had the hair for that thick, greased look with the combed duck's arse at the back.

A quick way to aggravate Henry was to call him an East Ender. I'm a Stepney boy, born in Cable Street, a quarter of a mile from Tower Bridge on the north side of the Thames. That is at the heart of the East End. Cross the Bridge into Bermondsey and you are into the Cooper territory of South-East London. The real East End takes in just Stepney, including Aldgate, Mile End, Whitechapel and Wapping, Bethnal Green, Bow, a bit of Hackney and Poplar. East of that, you're an East Londoner. My generation of East Enders will tell you there is a geographical difference. 'You're riff-raff,' Henry used to tease. And I wasn't going to argue with him. 'We South Londoners are posh compared with you lot,' he'd say, possibly even meaning it.

Even in his beautifully delivered eulogy at Henry's funeral, Jimmy Tarbuck called him the pride of the East End. But why should Scouser Jimmy know any better? Perhaps I should explain to him that it's like calling an Evertonian a Liverpudlian.

What I always found disconcerting about being in the company of the Cooper twins and manager Jim Wicks is that they always talked in the third person, using the Royal 'we'. It was 'we' did this, 'we' are going to do that, 'we' will take care of it, he didn't hurt 'us', he's never met anybody who hits as hard as 'we' do. Henry and George really were as one at times. You would find them continually finishing each other's sentences, ordering the same food from the menu at the same time, saying things in unison, and laughing or protesting at identical moments.

I had enormous respect for George, who never once moaned or groaned about having to live in his more famous brother's shadow. Back in their amateur days, many good judges rated George the better prospect. He had a booming right hand that was even more potent than Enery's famed and feared left hook, the 'Ammer.

But George was never quite the same force after breaking his right hand in one of his last amateur contests. He was an unlucky fighter, suffering throughout his career with far worse eye cuts than those that handicapped Henry. To try and beat the curse, he had plastic surgery to take the edge off his protruding eyebrows, but he continued to be known in the trade as 'a bleeder'. He won forty-two out of sixty-four amateur contests, many of the defeats caused by cut eyes; he also had to battle to overcome the rheumatic fever that put him flat on his back in hospital for three months when he was sixteen.

George was obliged to change his name to Jim Cooper when he turned professional in 1954, because there was already a licence holder from Poplar called George Cooper. Jim/George... identical twin brother Henry... a Dad named Henry... Jim Wicks, who could never get anybody's name right, referring to himself as 'we' as if the twins were triplets. It's a wonder George/Jim didn't have an identity crisis.

There was never a time when George gave me anything less than 100 per cent support. When we were boxing on the same bill, I always used to insist that I went on first because I got too nervous when he was fighting.

His right hand was the cat's whiskers. Gawd help anybody who got in its way when it was really travelling. He knew the boxing game inside out and was often in my corner, giving good advice and always keeping a cool head in a crisis.

We worked at Smithfield meat market for a while, carrying huge slabs of meat about on our shoulders. That was really hard graft, but the early morning shifts fitted in nicely with our training. Then we tried our hand at plastering, and that suited us down to the ground, or perhaps that should be up to the ceiling. I used the trowel with my left hand and George with his right. We would start on opposite sides of a room and meet in the middle of the ceiling. Nobody could finish plastering a ceiling quicker than we Coopers. I reckon that helped build our power. They used to say that between us we had Popeye's arms, because my left arm and George's right arm bulged with more muscle than our other arms.

George was reckoned by everybody who employed him to be a true artist of a plasterer. I used to just bish-bosh it on, but he went in for the fancy stuff – swirls, stipples, fans, that sort of thing – and you could have hung his work in a gallery. He married Barbara, the daughter of Reg Reynolds, who taught us all there is to know about the plastering game. So George did more than all right out of plastering. And before you make any jokes, we never once came home plastered. Throughout our boxing careers George and I rarely touched a drop of alcohol and neither of us went near tobacco until after we'd packed up boxing.

In fact the only booze we drank was a dreadful cocktail recommended by Jim Wicks. It was a mix of port and Guinness, and Jim used to encourage us to have it occasionally because he reckoned it was good for the constitution. Said he'd learned it from old-time fighters around about the First World War period when he was a good scrapper and had a few fairground bouts. Many years later when I started to suffer from gout I blamed it on that drink of Jim's! You should have seen the faces George and me pulled when we used to down the drink in one go. The Thomas a Becket pub, over which Jim had his office, was a Courage house and we used to say we needed courage to drink the Wicks cocktail.

Tell you what, nobody has a better brother than George. He's always there for me and me for him. I always used to jokingly put him in his place by saying I was the older and wiser one, but in truth we were bang equal in everything. Funny, but I could never really whack hard with my right hand, and George couldn't break eggs with his left. In fact, I reckon I would have been a southpaw if my early coaches had not insisted on me leading with my left. Now if I'd had George's right hand to go with my left hook, I think – no, I know – I would have done even better in my career.

George could whack every bit as hard as me, maybe even harder when that right hand of his was at its most potent. With just a little luck, he might easily have been a world champion. He was that good, but the old mince pies let him down big time.

The twins had their education interrupted by the war years, during which their council house in Fermstead Road, Bellingham took a hit, but the boys were by then safely evacuated to Lancing in Sussex. They left the local Athelney Road school at fifteen, more Philistines than Einsteins but street smart to degree level. Both Henry and George had got off to a less than distinguished start to their careers when boxing in the vest of the Bellingham Amateur Boxing Club. They each lost their first four schoolboy contests and both showed a worrying weakness against body shots. Bob Hill, a local fire brigade boxing champion who had recommended they take up the sport, was mystified. He then discovered that before each bout, both Henry and George were fed huge bread puddings by their mum, Lily, who thought this was helping them be strong, instead of sluggish and unable to take hard punches to the stomach.

Once they got their diet sorted out, they began to make their mark as amateurs. The slightly heavier George eventually boxed in the heavyweight division, leaving Henry to boil down to make light-heavyweight, because they had sworn never to fight each other.

In 1952, aged just seventeen and now boxing for the Eltham and District Amateur Boxing Club, Henry won a coveted ABA title and retained it the following year when he beat the highly acclaimed Australian Tony Madigan, who was later to give one Cassius Marcellus Clay a close call in the 1960 Rome Olympics.

But while developing into a celebrated amateur boxer on the domestic front, Henry did not travel well, failing to make an impact in his two major international tournaments overseas. Many thought he was robbed in his only contest in the 1952 Olympics in Helsinki, when he was adjudged to have been outpointed by Russian Anatoli Perov. The following year he competed in the European champion-ships in Warsaw. By then he was Lance-Corporal Henry Cooper of the Royal Army Ordnance Corps, otherwise known as the Boxers' Battalion. Corporal Cooper came up against a huge Russian bear called Juri Jegorow and suffered a public execution. He was giving away height and reach, and was stopped in the first round, his legs doing an involuntary dance after the Russian had landed a booming right to the jaw. It gave a new meaning to corporal punishment.

'The ref was right to stop it,' honest Henry acknowledged. 'I was not in a position to properly defend myself and could have taken a real tanking. I moaned at the time, but that was just me pride talking. Deep down I knew I'd got off lightly.'

Henry won seventy-three of eighty-four amateur bouts and was a regular in England and Great Britain vests. Among his opponents was his close pal in the Army, Joe Erskine, with whom he was to have one of the most exciting and exacting serials in British boxing history. They met three times as amateurs, Henry winning two-one. It was a friendly yet fierce rivalry that was to spill over into the professional arena with – as you will learn later – a near-disastrous climax to one of their fights.

We loved our amateur careers. This was in an era when it was every bit as popular as the pro game and we used to get full houses for the top competitions. There was great inter-club rivalry and the highlights were the divisional, London and national championships, and you would get to box at the main venues like the Albert Hall and Wembley Pool, and it was often on the telly. Me and George were local heroes and enjoyed the buzz of it all.

My only disappointment is that I didn't cover myself in glory in the two major events. Looking back, I realise I was too young. I was still a baby of eighteen when the Olympics took place in Helsinki in 1952. They were probably the hottest Games ever in boxing and very political because the Iron Curtain was as its most menacing and the Russians – professional in everything but name – refused to live in the Olympic village. My contest with Perov, a big unsmiling geezer who could have haunted houses for a living, was nip and tuck, and I thought I'd nicked it with my left jab that was never out of his wide face. I had two Eastern European judges vote against me and the French judge called me the winner. So out I went, beaten on a split decision by a mature man while I was still just a kid.

The Americans had a fantastic team, including future world stars of the calibre of Floyd Patterson, Spider Webb and Nate Brooks. The Hungarians had Laszlo Papp, the South Africans the Toweel brothers, and the Swedes Ingemar Johansson, who got himself slung out in the final for allegedly not trying. He later made them eat their words!

If we could have made a living out of it like the Iron Curtain boys we would have been happy to stay amateur, but you can't eat cups and medals, so George and me turned pro as soon as we escaped from the Army.

After their final amateur contests in April 1954, Henry and George honoured their pledge to sign as professionals with Jim Wicks. They had been introduced to him before starting their National Service by London *Evening News* boxing writer J. T. (Jimmy) Hulls, who liked the Cooper boys and said he wanted them to be in safe hands. Jim Wicks looked after them as carefully and as caringly as if they were precious porcelain china.

The Bishop already had a star-studded stable featuring such top-of-the-bill fighters as British light-heavyweight champion Alex Buxton, Empire bantamweight title-holder Jake Tuli and British lightweight king Joe Lucy.

The twins signed just one three-year contract with Wicks, which was never renewed. Both Henry and George were happy to let The Bishop manage them on word of honour only. It was as close to a father and sons' trust as you could get. Jim did not pay them signing-on money and just supplied them with satin shorts and dressing-gowns adorned with their names on the back. Other boxers accepted upfront money from unscrupulous managers, who would then make matches with a view to getting their money back rather than with the best interests of their boxers at heart. Jim Wicks was crafty but never a crook. The twins could not be in better hands.

A couple of years before signing the Coopers, Wicks had declined to sign another pair of twins, who were causing something of a stir across the water in the East End. They were Reggie and Ronnie Kray, both of whom had short professional careers before concentrating on using violence outside the ring to make their fortune.

I asked Henry if he knew them. 'Of course I did,' he said. 'You couldn't be in the boxing game and not be aware of them. They used to come and watch me train and would sit ringside for my fights. But that was as far as it went, although I did appear at a few charity events for them. Their villainy got all the headlines, but they did put something back into the community. In truth, we wanted nothing to do with them. I remember matchmaker Mickey Duff telling me he had banned them from becoming members of his Anglo-American Sporting Club at the London Hilton and the next week his wife opened a parcel hand-delivered to their door. Inside was a dead rat. Charming people.'

Henry listened politely to my story about my connection with the Krays, raised just half a mile down the road from me in Bethnal Green. In the 1960s they were looking to improve their public image and put the word around that they wanted a public relations adviser. A bit like Jack the Ripper seeking a media makeover.

Peter Batt, another Stepney-born sportswriter, and I got on to the shortlist, but were beaten to the job by Fred Dinenage, later of *How* TV show fame. Afterwards I discovered that I failed the interview because Reggie thought – blush, blush – I was too pretty (it was in my skinny, twenty-something days) and would be a distraction to gay Ronnie, who was having a fling at the time with the bisexual Lord Boothby. It was Fred Dineage who was in charge of the publicity when an infamous Sunday newspaper photograph was published of Boothby with the Krays, causing a political storm.

When I told all this to Henry he said: 'Fred Dinenage got the job? How?'

That was Aitch, always with the witty punchline.

FIRST PROFESSIONAL PUNCHES

Jim Wicks not only knew his boxers, horses, greyhounds and playing cards, he was also a master of public relations in an era when if you didn't beat the drum you went unnoticed and unheard, because there were few sports television programmes to carry the message to the masses. 'It's no good being a shrinking violation in this game, son,' he once told me, without any hint that he knew he was mangling a cliché.

In the 1950s, BBC Television had a flagship midweek show called *Sportsview*, which was presented by a creative pioneer producer named Peter Dimmock, a wartime RAF pilot who was terribly English and always wore a starched collar, and was immaculately groomed as if he had stepped out of a Savile Row tailor's shop window.

It would be difficult to imagine two more contrasting people than Dimmock and The Bishop. This was Mr Pickwick meeting the Artful Dodger. They were separated by a common language, but Jim worked his Cockney charm on the BBC sports boss and persuaded him to feature the Cooper twins signing professional contracts live on air.

It could only be 'live' in those days because recording facilities were in their infancy. Jim told me years later in his Arfur Daley tones: 'I just had a word in Mr Dimmock's shell-like and told him I was about to sign boxing's equivalent of the Beverley Sisters, who were the biggest act in town at the time.'

The stunt drew more publicity than even Jim envisioned, when the studio ring in which Henry and George were sparring with each other collapsed. Neither of the twins was hurt and they clambered out of the wreckage to sign British Boxing Board of Control contracts in front of the cameras.

As the boys switched to the professional ranks, they brought with them their highly rated Eltham ABC trainer Georgie Page, who had been a top-flight amateur boxer before becoming a dedicated coach. The plan was for George to work in harness with Danny Holland on their fitness and tactics. But Page was at heart a diehard, dedicated amateur and the shenanigans of the professional game were against all he stood for; so it was not long before he quit to return to his first love of youth boxing and training the stars of the future.

The twins both made winning debuts in down-the-bill six-round-ers at Harringay Arena on 14 September 1954. This was long before Harringay became Haringey. Henry floored veteran Harry Painter twice in the first round with the left hook that was to bring him fame and fortune, and the referee counted out an opponent who at 14st 13lb was more than a stone heavier than Our Enery. Being outweighed would become the norm for Henry. In only eight fights throughout his career did he have a weight advantage.

George had a tougher scrap in his debut, surviving a brutal butt-ing attack before winning on points against a wild young Welsh giant called Dick Richardson, who would figure in Henry's future fight programme.

Me and George felt like millionaires that night. We shared £70 plus £35 expenses. Dear old Jim did not take his percentage, and it was a couple of years before he did collect the 25 per cent cut he was entitled to. It would have taken four weeks or more to earn that kind of dosh plastering.

We went out next morning and bought Mum and Dad their first television set, a thirty quid black-and-white Pye with a nine-inch screen that you had to watch in a darkened room, and with a giant H-shape aerial on the roof that looked as if it could have collected signals from Mars. It was state of the art then and there was only the one BBC channel. I remember sitting watching presenters McDonald Hobley in a dickie bow and Sylvia Peters in a ball gown and feeling undressed without a tie on.

We just wanted to show our appreciation to Mum and Dad for the way they'd always got behind us and encouraged us. Life had been really tough for them. Dad worked on the trams and then cleaning out furnaces, and never earned more than eight quid a week, and Mum slaved as a charlady to help feed Bernie, George and me in the wartime and ration book days. We were hungry young hounds, as you can imagine. We weren't exactly tiny chaps, were we! Fancy having to feed and clothe us. Gawd knows how they managed it, but they did.

George and me used to wear hand-me-downs from big brother Bernie and used to go through shoes in weeks because we were always kicking stones around if we couldn't get a ball to kick, and we were forever tearing our clothes while clambering around the bomb-blitzed buildings near the docks. Back in those days I was dreaming of following either my idol Joe Louis as a boxer or England goalie Frank Swift as a goalkeeper. I was useful between the sticks and got to play in goal for South London schoolboys, but boxing won out in the end because George was as mad on it as I was, so we settled on fighting rather than football. Think we chose well, because footballers back then were only earning about seventeen quid a week, not like today's millionaire players.

Mum worked miracles during the war. Dad was away fighting in Burma and she brought us up on her own for nearly four years. She could be as tough as Dad with the old discipline bit. If we misbehaved she would clip us round the ear, and if that didn't work she'd take her shoe off and tan our arses. As kids, you don't realise at the time how tough it must have been for your parents. Looking back on it, Mum deserved a medal for the way she managed while Dad was doing his bit for King and Country. As George and I started to earn from our boxing, we were able to repay our parents for all the sacrifices they'd made to bring us up. They did a fair old job considering everything.

Henry took his love of his parents to the extreme of having 'Mum and Dad' tattooed on his left arm. I don't think I was the first boxing scribe to describe his left jabs and hooks as giving his opponents a mummy and a daddy of a hiding.

His professional career got off to a promising start, with nine straight wins in seven months, all but two inside the distance and including an impressive eight rounds points win over the huge Birkenhead-based Jamaican Joe Bygraves. 'Jolting Joe', built like a brick outhouse, had turned professional within days of chinning a referee who had disqualified him during a Wales v. England international. The same referee had earlier disqualified Henry, who responded with a more sedate shrug of the shoulders. Bygraves would come back to haunt (and hurt) our hero.

The Cooper style of boxing had not changed noticeably from his amateur days. He was still as upright as a guardsman and advanced from behind a rat-a-tat-tat left-hand lead that was the precursor for a left hook that was always delivered with venom. His right hand was held high, protecting his chin from counters, and he would use it sparingly, mostly as a supplement to a sudden burst of combination punches perfected on the speedball in the gymnasium. His favourite blend was a short left to the ribs, bringing down his opponent's guard, and then an instant left hook to the jaw. When it worked to perfection it was like violent poetry, but for the opponent on the receiving end nothing rhymed. One of his specialities that he produced throughout his career was a left hook counter, delivered while drawing his opponent forward and with his weight on his back foot, then suddenly shifted to the front to give what he described as a car-collision impact as the punch landed on the jaw of his advancing adversary.

Henry and George could have put on a Vaudeville act with their side-by-side synchronised rope skipping, and both could get up on their toes and dance around the ring, but for their big punches they used to plant their feet for maximum impact.

Taking on his first Continental opponent in his tenth fight, a red curtain descended on Cooper's world and it was a portent of things to come. He was well in command against Italian champion Uber Bacilieri when a clash of heads midway through the second round opened a deep gash on his left eyebrow. Jim Wicks called the fight off as soon as Henry returned to his corner at the bell. It was not that the cut was so bad as Jim not wanting to risk further damage. 'We couldn't see out of the eye because of the blood,' 'triplet' Jim reported afterwards. 'It's a pity because we were in great shape and well on top. It would have been insanitary for us to carry on.' Jim, of course, meant insanity.

Henry quickly got back to winning ways once the eye had healed, and in his twelfth fight avenged his defeat by Bacilieri at London's White City on 13 September 1955, knocking the Italian cold in the seventh round. 'We knew we could take him out anytime but wanted to get a few rounds under our belt,' said The Bishop. 'Yeah, yeah, yeah,' said Henry.

It was unlucky thirteenth for Henry when he was narrowly outpointed over ten rounds by his old foe Joe Erskine in an eliminator for the British heavyweight title at Harringay Arena on 15 November 1955.

In these days of monster heavyweights, it seems incredible that Henry was fretting that he was coming into the ring too heavy at 13st 11lb.

My best fighting weight was a few ounces either side of 13st 6lb. I know it sounds ridiculous that a couple of pounds can make a difference, but I was finding out that if I went into the ring at, say, more than 13–9 I was sluggish and unable to get into my rhythm.

I dared not carry any extra pounds against a wily old git like Joe, who was the cleverest and craftiest boxer I ever met. I used to tell him he boxed like he played cards. We played for hours when in the Army together, and when he was holding the pack he had a sleight of hand that somehow ghosted just the card he wanted on to the table. I couldn't kick up a fuss because I could never prove he was doing it, but I used to say to him, 'You should belong to the Magic Circle, Joe.' And that was how he boxed – now you see me, now you don't.

He was an absolute master at making you hit thin air and for a card shark he had the perfect poker face. You never knew what he was thinking or whether you had hurt him with a punch. His expression just never changed from one round to the next. If he had been able to punch his weight he would definitely have won a world title. Him beating us in that vital eliminator was the biggest choker we'd had in our career to date. Meantime, George was having problems with recurring cut eyes, and so that was a low time for us and we had to work at trying to lift each other's spirits. We were both still living at home with Mum and Dad and a blanket of gloom dropped over our little house.

George had sharper, more protruding cheekbones and eyebrows, and leaked blood in virtually every fight. He eventually went into Queen Victoria Hospital at East Grinstead, where a plastic surgeon sort of planed the edge off his eyebrows. But sadly for George it did not really cure his problem.

It could easily have been that the press were reporting the death rather than the defeat of Henry after his points loss to Erskine. Driving home after the fight in their old, second-hand Ford Prefect, the twins were involved in a terrifying crash, and to make it worse big brother Bernie and his pregnant wife, Cory, were passengers in the back. They collided with a huge Wolseley at a crossroads in Hackney and the car somersaulted twice, with the Coopers trapped inside. Miraculously nobody was seriously hurt, but the driver of the Wolseley did a double take when he saw Henry climb out of the wreckage with his face still bruised and bloodied from his losing fight with Joe. 'We were lucky as hell to survive the crash,' Henry said. 'Our only concern was for Cory and the unborn baby. She had a check-up and everything was all right. Scared the life out of us all, but we later had a good laugh at the look on the other driver's face when he clocked my cuts and bruises!'

Henry quickly restored his reputation and ranking in his fifteenth fight, with a sensational first round victory over 'Blackpool Rock' Brian London, who had won the 1954 Empire Games heavyweight title in Vancouver, boxing as Brian Harper. When turning professional he took the ring surname of his father Jack London, who had been a British professional heavyweight champion in the immediate post-war years. Always shooting from the lip, Brian had made no secret of what he intended to do to Cooper. He had rushed to twelve victories since turning professional, eleven of his wins coming in quick time. Henry had beaten his brother, Jack, as an amateur and Brian had stopped George Cooper in four rounds as a pro, so it was a real family feud when rookie promoter Freddie Mills brought them together at the Empress Hall on May Day 1956.

The fight was barely a minute old when Henry had London sending out distress signals. He made him grunt with a short right to the body and London momentarily dropped his hands. That was like sending a gilt-edged invitation for Henry's left hook, which he smashed against London's unguarded jaw with such force that it knocked him back into the ring post in a neutral corner. He was out on his feet, propped up against the post, and as Henry unleashed a string of combination punches the referee jumped in and led the outgunned and out-to-the-world London back to the safety of his corner.

'We like to do our fighting with our fists, not our mouths,' declared The Bishop. 'Brian said some very naughty things about us and we had to make him pay for it. Now we want to be considered back in contention for the top titles.' Over to Henry: 'Whatever Jim says we'll do, yeah.' They were the best double act in boxing.

The confidence of the Cooper camp evaporated before the year was out when Yorkshire heavyweight prospect Peter Bates opened the left eye wound again to force a fifth round stoppage after Henry had dropped him for a nine count and was just waiting to deliver the *coup de grâce*.

Then came Henry's *annus horribilis*, a year in which he seriously considered hanging up his gloves. He became disillusioned after three title fight defeats in succession in 1957.

The first setback was against Joe Bygraves, whom he had outpointed two years earlier. This time the British Empire title was up for grabs and the Cooper camp made the mistake of sending Henry into the ring at his heaviest ever, 13st 13lb, to try and counter the Incredible Bulk that was Bygraves. Aitch (that's what his Cockney pals called him) fought that night at Earls Court as if he was on sinking sand rather than a ring canvas. There was no snap in his punches and his footwork was more Old Mother Kelly than Gene Kelly.

In the ninth round, with the scorecards even, Bygraves threw a short right from close range that caught Henry in the solar plexus. The punch literally took his breath away and he collapsed to his knees, gasping for air, as the referee tolled the ten-second count. Jim Wicks, his face longer than a bishop's cassock, told the press: 'We couldn't breathe. If we'd stayed on our feet it would've been even worse, so we dropped to our knees. It was just a freak punch. We'll be back.' Henry nodded, 'We'll be back, yeah.'

Next stop Stockholm and a European title challenge against the handsome, dimpled Swede Ingemar Johansson, who had won his sixteen professional fights to date but had many doubters, who considered him too cautious to make it to the top. Blackening his CV was a controversial performance in the 1952 Olympics, when he had suffered the humiliation of being disqualified for 'not giving of his best'. Johansson appeared to have frozen with fear and did not throw a punch in the final against American giant Ed Sanders. He was literally running away around the ring, and eventually the referee spread his arms and declared enough of one of the most embarrassing exhibitions ever seen in an Olympic ring. Years later Ingemar had the disqualification expunged from the records, when his explanation that he was trying to draw Sanders on to a counter punch was finally accepted.

Ingemar was an unashamed playboy, who took his girlfriend to his training camps and said he put all his faith in his 'toonder and lightning' right hand, Ingo's Bingo.

Strangely enough, his fight with Henry was taking a similar pattern to the notorious Olympic final. Ingemar hardly threw a punch for the first four rounds and as Henry had decided he would also use counter punching tactics it was becoming a toothless tango. Both boxers circled around the ring without any risk or danger of making physical contact as the sun set over the open-air arena on a beautiful May evening in Stockholm. Over to Henry:

The crafty so-and-sos saw to it that I had the corner facing the setting sun and I was blinded for much of the fight. That's not an excuse, that is fact.

If I'd paid to see the fight I'd have been asking for my money back after four rounds of nothing more exciting than shadow boxing. It was weird because there was so little atmosphere in the enormous stadium that I could hear the conversations of ringsiders.

Like a mug, I got impatient and decided to change my tactics and go after Johansson. Big mistake. As I went forward in the fifth round hunting him, he drew me towards the setting sun. I could not see a thing and then b-o-o-m he let his looping right hand go. The next I knew I was down on my knees in a kneeling position and by the time I scrambled up the referee was shouting 'Nine, ten... Out.' Bleedin' Bingo!

Apart from amateurish flicking left hands, it was about the only punch he threw in the fight. I felt more embarrassed than hurt because we'd not had a proper fight. Of course, a couple of years later he goes and does the same thing to Floyd Patterson and wins the world title. Ingemar was a real charmer out of the ring but, let's be honest, he was not the best of world champions. All he had was that right hand, but what a punch – and it made him a fortune.

Never having been knocked out in my life – my boxing career ended with two broken wrists in an East London schoolboys' championship contest that I won – I asked Henry what it was like. 'You know as much as me,' he said. 'The lights go out, and when you come round you wonder what hit you. When the punch is to the jaw you don't even feel any pain, and the next thing you know you're on the floor and the ref is counting over you, and you wonder why your legs won't obey you. The worst knockout for me was when Joe Bygraves landed that punch to my solar plexus. Your breath just leaves you and for a moment you cannot help but panic, wondering whether you're going to get your breath back. One thing I know is that I preferred giving rather than receiving!'

The heartbreak hat-trick of defeats that best-forgotten year was completed by Joe Erskine, who successfully defended the British heavyweight title he had taken from Johnny Williams with a narrow fifteen rounds points victory over Henry at Harringay Arena on 15 September 1957. This gave him a 3–2 lead in their series since first meeting as amateurs. For all their thumping of each other, they remained good pals and Henry was sporting enough to say after his defeat: 'Good luck to Joe. I hope he goes on and takes the European and world titles. He's good enough.'

Henry kept to himself that he was depressed to the point that he was considering throwing in the towel and going back to taking up the trowel. He was still living at home with his parents, was leading the Spartan life of the dedicated sportsman, did not drink or smoke, allowed no distraction from the opposite sex, trained consistently and conscientiously and here he was, a four-times-on-the-trot loser. Meanwhile, his brother George was proving he could make as much money plastering as fighting, and the trowel did not hit you back.

After stewing at home for a month, Henry realised he could not do without boxing. He was literally hooked on it.

Henry phoned The Bishop and said he was ready to get back into the ring.

'I knew you'd come to that conclusion, Enery,' Jim told him. 'I've arranged a nice little trip for us. We're going to Germany.'

HENRY ÜBER ALLES

Even with all his Barnum and Bailey blarney, Jim Wicks could not cajole home promoters into using Henry after his four successive defeats. It would have been easier to sell ice lollies to Eskimos.

So Jim broadened his horizons and arranged for Henry to fight away from critical British eyes against German champion Hans Kalbfell in Dortmund on 16 November 1957. Suddenly Henry was cast in the role of journeyman, and only a victory could save him from the ignominious slide towards fighting purely for money and being 'the opponent'.

Kalbfell stood 6ft 4in tall, looked as if he had been hewn out of German granite and had more than a stone weight advantage. He was being groomed for a world title challenge, and his promoters and supporters saw Henry as just a stepping stone. Instead, our hero stepped all over Kalbfell. He boxed his ears off with a magnificent display of controlled aggression, dominating the ten-round fight from first bell to last.

British soldiers based in Germany invaded the ring and trium-phantly carried Henry shoulder-high around it after he had been confirmed as the runaway points winner, and the consensus was this was his finest performance to date. 'We have never boxed better,' said Jim Wicks. 'We were wunderbra.'

Our Enery was back in demand. In Germany.

The victory did not generate a lot of press coverage in Britain, so Jim put his thinking cap on and came up with a story that made huge headlines: 'OUR ENERY UNDER HYPNOSIS'.

He revealed that Henry was being hypnotised by a German professor, who was teaching him how to relax, and that he was now ready to become a world-beater. Substance was given to the story when Henry was spotted making several private visits to Germany.

The fact was that he had met a pretty Fräulein called Hilda and had a brief relationship with her. It suited him to say he was going to Germany for hypnosis sessions.

The Bishop was no mere spin doctor, more a spin surgeon. He would go to any lengths to publicise a fight. Jim managed a South African flyweight called Jake Tuli, who he had photographed with a spear and billed as Zulu Jake Tuli, telling tales of his warrior deeds. Jake had never seen a spear in his life before celebrated South London sports photographer Derek Rowe handed him one for the promotion photo.

To get early-career publicity for the twins, Jim once leaked a story that he had turned down an offer of £50,000 for their contracts, at a time when that was a small fortune. He said the offer had come from a syndicate headed by film actor Stanley Baker, a great fan and friend of Henry's who stood the story up although there was not even a germ of truth in it. Jim later confided that a bookmaker had offered to take Henry and George off his hands in settlement of a five grand betting debt. The Bishop preferred to pay up rather than lose the two boys he looked upon as sons.

Another of Jim's nicknames was Seamus, because of his Irish family background and the fact that he was full of blarney. When he signed Tuli, he told the press he had a soft spot for South Africa because he had visited there as a boy drummer during the Boer War. It was published as fact, with nobody bothering to check that the war finished when Jim was just six. The Bishop, who kept the company of vagabonds and princes, told lots of porkies, but if you could give him a winner in the next race at Haydock Park, you were a friend for life.

Jim literally would gamble on two flies climbing up the window-pane and he had scores of tales about his days as a bookmaker when it was illegal to bet away from a racecourse. He told stories of shady associates switching horses to pull off betting coups, nobbling favourites and bribing jockeys to pull their mounts. Probably one in three stories was true, but he was always entertaining to listen to and he used to have the Cooper twins (and gullible young reporters like me) hanging on his every word. There will never be another like The Bishop. My father George Giller was a bookie's street runner at the same time that Jim was working the racecourses. This, of course, was in the days before betting shops and Dad's illegal job was to collect pencil-written bets from punters he met in pubs and doorways and then run them to the bookmaker in time for the bets to be laid. Among his paymasters was a Billingsgate fishmonger called Jack Solomons, later to become the self-styled Czar of British boxing promoters and who had been shown the bookmaking ropes by Jim Wicks.

The people making the bets, ranging from housewives, dockers and labourers to lawyers, policemen and schoolteachers, never put their real names on the slips, but used nicknames or *noms de plume*. I used to sign mine as Redwing, after one of my favourite old jazz tunes. Henry considered betting a mug's game and used to shake his head in disbelief when watching his manager win hundreds of pounds during the course of a meal then lose it all again just as quickly. Jim would shrug and be back in action the next day. Many bookmakers, including Jack Solomons and The Bishop, were all but put out of business the day in 1946 when 50–1 outsider Airborne won the Epsom Derby. It was considered a donkey, but romped home carrying the wagers of thousands of recently demobbed servicemen attracted by the name, plus the punts of many house-wives putting their sixpences on the grey. My dad's bookie boss was ruined by the result and he hanged himself, unable to repay his debts.

Back to the Henry story and to Dortmund for fight number twenty-two on 11 January 1958. In the opposite corner, the recently dethroned European heavyweight champion Heinz Neuhaus, who was rebuilding his career on a run of victories over British-based boxers Peter Bates, Brian London and .Joe Bygraves. Neutral observers agreed that Henry won at least seven of the ten rounds against the lumbering Neuhaus. The result: a draw! Even the German fans booed the decision and chanted Henry's name. The Bishop found the right word: 'Diabolical.'

Henry's love affair with Germany (and also with Hilda) ended in Frankfurt on 19 April 1958, when he was disqualified in the sixth round against the highly regarded Erich Schoeppner – after the referee had counted out the unconscious German light-heavyweight champion and raised Cooper's hand in victory.

Schoeppner had half turned his back as Henry mounted an attack and a left hook thundered against his ear with such force that he was stretchered out of the ring and hospitalised for five weeks. Officials of the German Boxing Federation put their heads together and decided Our Enery had won with an illegal rabbit punch and named the unconscious Schoeppner the winner and fined Cooper half his £1,500 purse.

This time the apoplectic Bishop was almost lost for words. But not quite. He leaned on one of the oldest laments in boxing: 'We woz robbed.'

They stitched us up like a kipper. There was no way it was a deliberate foul. Schoeppner was backing off and turned away from me just as I let the old left hook go. It was aimed at the side of his jaw, but as he turned it landed on his ear, not on the back of his neck, which would have been a rabbit punch.

Poor old Erich knew nothing about what was going on. He was out to the world. That should have gone down on our record as a knock-out victory. To disqualify us was bad enough, but then to take half our money just rubbed it in. Jim really laid into the promoters in the dressing-room afterwards and nearly started World War Three. We were choked and Jim made it clear we would never fight in Germany again. I never saw Hilda after that.

Next up, Henry was delivered for sacrifice – so many people thought – against fast-rising Welshman Dick Richardson on his own manor of Porthcawl on 3 September 1958. Dick, 6ft 4in of fearsome second row forward, had been terrorising the heavyweight division with his roughhouse tactics and it was thought he would be too strong and aggressive for Our Enery.

Perhaps it was fitting that the fight was staged on the anniversary of the outbreak of the Second World War because Richardson started as if he was a tank going into battle. He charged at Henry, butting him back across the ring and opening a jagged cut on his eyebrow. Cuts man Danny Holland had to work overtime between rounds to stem the flow of blood and as he sent him out for round five, the blood-stained Bishop told him: 'We can't go on much more. The cut's getting worse and we'll have to pull out. It's now or never, my son.'

Sensing that Cooper was in trouble, Richardson – a notorious street fighter – came out with both fists flailing and with his head coming through as a third weapon. He caught Henry with a swinging right that knocked him down on to his haunches. Henry mouthed to The Bishop in the corner that he was all right, but Richardson thought he was signalling that he was in trouble.

The Welsh warrior came charging at Henry as he got up at the count of eight with the one idea of ending the fight there and then. He achieved his objective to some degree. Henry met him with a left hook of such force that it lifted the sixteen-stone giant off his feet and sent him crashing down and out. It was one of the most awesome one-punch finishes seen in a British ring for years.

'We've never hit anybody so hard,' said The Bishop. 'This will frighten the life out of all our rivals. We're now an illegitimate contender for the titles.'

When film of the exciting fight and its finale was shown on television Henry's popularity lifted to the sky, and never really came down again.

Major things were happening on the British boxing front. Jack Solomons, for many years the number one promoter, was having his monopoly challenged by a new team – some called it a syndicate – headed by Harry Levene, with wealthy entrepreneur Jarvis Astaire and ex-fighter and matchmaker Mickey Duff, and future William Hill boss Sam Burns in support.

It was a fierce and bitter rivalry, and The Bishop took great delight in feeding off it. He knew he had the ace calling card in Henry

Cooper, and played Solomons and Levene off against each other with all the skill of a Malcolm Sargent conducting the Last Night at the Proms.

Solomons thought he could count on Wicks because of a friendship going back to the 1930s, when Jim taught him all about the bookmaking game. Levene thought he could count on Wicks because he employed his son, Jackie Wicks, as a hugely efficient promotions organiser. But The Bishop's loyalty belonged only to his boxers, and he made Solomons and Levene battle it out with chequebooks. Henry's bank account was the winner.

I had better own up here to what could be seen as vested interest. For several years I worked as a publicist for Messrs Levene, Astaire and Duff (also for my best mate, the late Terry Lawless, and at the Albert Hall for Mike Barrett), but at this stage – as the first shots were being fired in the promotional war – I was a young *Boxing News* scribe more interested in reporting punches than politics.

On 14 October 1958 Levene was forced to pay Henry's highest purse to date – £7,500 – for him to top the bill at Wembley Arena – then known as Wembley Pool – against world-ranked Alex Miteff. Two weeks before the fight the Argentine pulled out with an injury and Levene told Wicks: 'You have a choice of substitute opponent… Zora Folley or Sonny Liston.' Both of them were in training and ready to take Cooper on at short notice.

Jim the Joker came up with a quote that has been enshrined in fight folklore: 'We don't want anything to do with that mahogany wardrobe Liston. We don't want to be in the same room as him, let alone the same ring. He is an animal.'

The fearsome, ex-jailbird Liston was still two years from ripping the world title away from Floyd Patterson, but had already built up a reputation for being a fighter to avoid at all costs.

So Wicks settled for Zora Folley, one of the most stylish and skilled of all the world title contenders and rated No. 3 for the crown held by 'Freudian Floyd' (who after his defeat by Johansson was so ashamed that he left the stadium disguised with a beard).

Henry got off to a dodgy start against the accomplished Folley, walking into his left hand for three rounds and taking a nine count after being caught by a snap right cross. But Folley then forgot his basic boxing ability and went all out for a knockout and his punches were suddenly being telegraphed. This brought the best out of Henry's rhythmic boxing style and he continually slipped inside Folley's swinging right hands and jabbed his opponent almost to a standstill with a procession of thumping lefts. Jim Wicks summed it up beautifully: 'We made him eat our left hand for breakfast.'

It was an amazing transformation and Henry went on to a resounding ten rounds points victory that earned him a standing ovation from the sell-out Wembley crowd. The performance underlined Henry's new standing as a world championship contender and he had now won respect on both sides of the Atlantic.

This is where I came in as something more than a fan and spectator, with my first interview with Henry. After our early-morning road run together, described in the first chapter, he told me about his preparations for his upcoming challenge for Brian London's British and Empire championships.

London had taken the titles from Joe Erskine in the summer of 1958, when he knocked out the Welshman in the seventh round.

I put ten questions to Henry after our road run and all these years later his answers still make interesting reading and give an insight to Henry's thinking. His responses are delivered in the Royal 'we' style:

1. How big a psychological advantage is it that you stopped London in the first round the last time you met?

We don't believe in thinking about past fights. We'll let London dwell on what we did to him last time, but as far as we're concerned we're getting ourselves in nick to go the full fifteen rounds. If we can catch him early again, great. If not, we're prepared to go the distance, by which time we know he'll be sick to death of the old left hand.

2. Does George ever spar with you when you're training for a fight?

We do light stuff just for rhythm but never punch each other with full weight. I knocked out one of our sparring partners when I was training for the fight with Dick Richardson, and in emergency George put the gloves on to help me finish the sparring session. The silly sod caught me with a slashing right hand that cut my eye and we had to get a postponement. We would never ever fight each other for real.

3. How difficult is it to concentrate when you are handicapped by a cut eye?

It's a curse we've learned to live with. We used to get uptight until our manager Jim Wicks said to relax and let him and Danny Holland worry about it. Danny is the best cuts man in the business and we know that each time we get back to the corner he'll do a smashing job in patching me up. My brother George has a much worse time with cuts than I do. He would be challenging for championships if it weren't for his minces always giving him trouble.

4. You will probably be giving away at least a stone and a half to London. Does that bother you?

We've always believed in the old saying, 'The bigger they are, the harder they fall'. We like fighting bigger, heavier opponents. It usually means they are less mobile and we can beat them for speed and there's a bigger target to hit. If they're coming towards us and the old hook lands flush on the jaw it is like a collision of cars and we make twice the impact. That's what happened when we knocked out Dick Richardson. Thought he was going to take off for the Moon! He went at least a foot up into the air as we connected with one of the hardest punches we've ever thrown. To be able to do that to a guy of sixteen stone shows our power. Could almost feel Dick's chin on my knuckles for days afterwards.

5. This is something of a golden age for heavyweights. Not counting yourself, there's London, Richardson, Joe Erskine and Joe Bygraves. Who do you rate the best of them?

For skill, Joe Erskine by a mile. He is a very difficult opponent to pin with a punch, and can make you look a fool just by clever footwork and crafty body shifts. Just as well he can't punch his weight! If title fights were over eight rounds, Bygraves would be hard to beat, but he lacks real stamina because he is so heavily muscled. Richardson is just a bull in a china shop, but I wouldn't like to have to fight him on the cobbles. London is what we call in the game a good 'on top' fighter, but can be quickly put in his place if you show you're not going to be intimidated by his bullying tactics.

6. What do you consider your best performance to date?

Apart from our one-round stoppage of London, it has to be either our points victory over Hans Kalbfell in Dortmund last year or our win over Zora Folley, who many people were saying is the best heavyweight in the world at the moment. We've never boxed better than we did against Kalbfell. He hardly laid a glove on us for ten rounds. It was a vital victory for us after a run of four successive defeats that dented our confidence.

7. You seem to have a rapport with Jim Wicks that goes beyond the usual manager/boxer relationship.

Jim is like a second dad to us. It was the best thing we ever did, signing for him. He is always a cool and calculating head in the corner, matches us with care and makes sure we get the best possible financial deals. It's a tough old game and there are some unscrupulous managers around who take liberties with their boys, but Jim cares about us as if we're his own sons. If he were ever to retire we'd pack it in straight away. We wouldn't want anybody else managing us.

8. Who was your favourite fighter when you first started boxing?

It has to be the one and only Joe Louis. The Brown Bomber was very special in our household. My dad, who loves his boxing, swore he was the greatest heavyweight who ever lived. We all got our love of boxing passed down from our Granddad George, who was a well-known bare-knuckle fighter round the Elephant and Castle area. I suppose boxing's in our blood, really. Pound for pound, I would say Sugar Ray Robinson is the greatest fighter there's ever been, certainly of my lifetime.

9. You famously started out as a plasterer, do you still do any of that hard graft?

No, I gave it up after about eighteen months as a pro because I was getting too tired, what with all the training and fighting. But George has kept it up. He is a master plasterer, ask anybody who's seen his work. He did some plastering round our manager's place the other month. He's still not been paid. Put that in *Boxing News*. That'll give us a laugh! Jim's bound to read it. He only reads two papers, *Boxing News* and *The Sporting Life*.

10. What's your prediction for the London fight, and what would being champion mean to you?

We don't go shooting our mouth off like London. We see he's talking about stopping me to avenge what we did to him last time we met, but words are cheap. Let's just say we're confident the belts will be hung round our waist at the end and to win the titles will mean everything to us. It will make up for that horrible year we had in 1957 and it will prove wrong all those people who wrote us off as finished.

It's history that Henry outpointed London and won the British and Empire belts for the first time. Extraordinarily, he was to remain British champion for the next twelve years apart from when he briefly gave up the championship on a point of principle.

Many years later Henry confessed that this second meeting with London was one of the toughest fights of his life. His nose was cut in the first round and blood was running down into his throat from his nostrils throughout the fight, making breathing a challenge.

Henry managed to hide his crisis from London, an opponent of great fitness but little finesse. For fifteen viciously hard rounds he pumped his left jab into the Blackpool man's accommodating face. London, covered in both his own blood and Henry's, was so confused and bemused by the pummelling he was taking that at the end of the fourteenth round he held up Henry's arm in victory, not realising there was still another round to go. The Bishop's verdict: 'It was good of London to give us a half-time score. We won by the provincial mile.' And the proverbial one, too.

It was back to Porthcawl on 26 August 1959 for a defence of his Empire heavyweight title against Gawie de Klerk, a man mountain of a policeman from Johannesburg. The South African fought with courage but was out of his depth and the referee came to his rescue as

Henry opened up with a vicious volley of punches in the fifth round that had de Klerk staggering around like a blind man in a maze.

Henry's twenty-eighth professional contest – against his oldest rival Joe Erskine – was to cause him the fright of his life.

And it was his final fight as a single man.

ROUND 4

GLOVE STORY TO LOVE STORY

ove was just around the corner as Henry prepared to take on his great nemesis Joe Erskine in a fight that would almost certainly make or break one of them. He had fallen – slowly, it has to be said, like a tumbling oak tree – for a tiny Italian waitress at our mutually favourite Soho restaurant, Peter Mario's in Gerrard Street.

The waitress was one Albina Genepri, who had come to London from her home, a small farm in the foothills of the Apennines, to be educated and then work at her uncle's restaurant when she was sixteen. She was pretty and bubbly, barely five feet tall and spoke Chico Marx English. By the time Henry got round to courting her she was into her twenties and had enough command of the language to put us customers in our place with non-stop friendly banter.

To watch Albina and Henry falling in love was the stuff of Mills & Boon, and I am not talking Freddie Mills and Eric Boon.

By his own admission, Henry struggled to chat up girls. He lived for his boxing and was basically a shy man. You would never find him in a nightclub or a dancehall, and when training for fights he used to be in bed by nine-thirty ready for his 4.45 a.m. alarm call the next morning. The fling with Fräulein Hilda apart, he was close to chaste.

Our Enery epitomised how great sportsmen of his time gave 100 per cent to the pursuit of fitness. He grew up admiring dozens of champions who set the right example: Stanley Matthews and Billy Wright in football, Sir Len Hutton and Peter May in cricket, Henry Cotton and Arnold Palmer in golf. All his idols were clean-living and dedicated to their sport.

When he fell for Albina, a little matter of six years since she had started serving him his regular meal at Mario's, those of us looking on from the sidelines almost felt like applauding. We had long seen the sparks, but they seemed to fly over Henry's head.

I used to eat regularly at Mario's with my *Boxing News* colleagues Tim Riley and Ron Olver, and Albina was our waitress in the days shortly after she had left school in Clerkenwell and tried – and failed – her hand as a dressmaker. Henry had yet to clap eyes on her, and I always loved being able to tell him that I knew his wife before he did. We watched her grow into an elegant and confident young lady, who lit up the room with her personality and contagious laughter.

Mario's, standing out as an Italian restaurant in the heart of Chinatown, was a popular haunt for the boxing aficionados, with Jack Solomons's gym just a stroll away in a basement opposite the Windmill Theatre, and promoters, managers and matchmakers were always meeting at nearby Mario's to talk business. It was a great place for a journalist to pick up stories and gossip, and for me – a jazz lover – it had the extra pull of being just a few doors from Ronnie Scott's original jazz club. (Ronnie and I went to the same East End school, where he was then known as Ronnie Schatt. Could never understand why he changed his name.)

Jim Wicks, a gourmet who used to go through the menu with the

For King and for Queen and country. The Cooper twins (Henry, left) swore allegiance to King George VI when they started their National Service with the Army, and Queen Elizabeth II was on the throne by the time they were demobbed in 1953. It was forty-seven years later that Henry was knighted by the Queen.

Proud Mum Lily reads a congratulatory telegram after Henry – showing the signs of battle – had beaten world-ranked Zora Folley in 1958. George, as ever, gives his full support.

It is 1955 and the start of the five-fight professional rivalry between Henry and Joe Erskine. They shake hands at the weigh-in before a battle won over ten rounds by the Welsh boxing master, with Joe's manager Benny Jacobs looking on. Including their three contests as amateurs, they met each other eight times. Henry won the last three to come out top 5–3 in their two-man war; below is how it ended in their sixth duel, with Joe bent over the bottom rope like a giant violin bow.

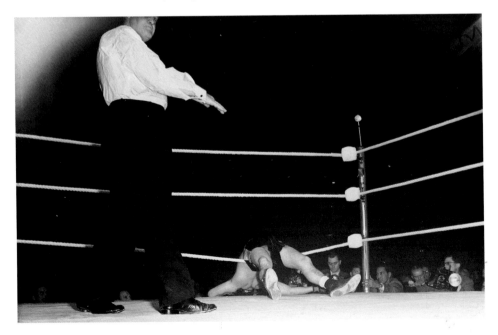

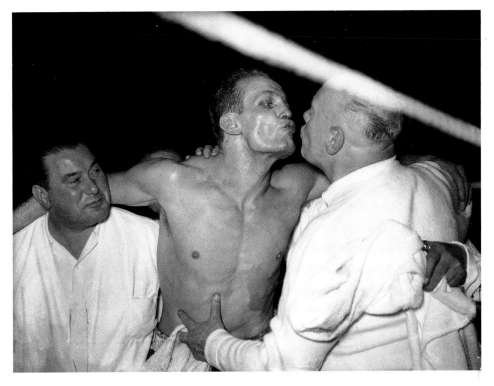

A kiss for Jim Wicks (above), with trainer Danny Holland looking on, perhaps enviously, and a right bang on the nose for Joe Erskine (below) in the British and Empire Heavyweight Championship contest that Henry won on a twelfth-round stoppage at Earls Court in 1959.

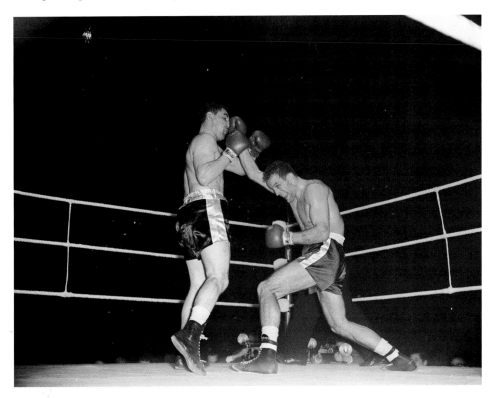

Henry the 'Mean Machine' beating Newport giant Dick Richardson for a second time in five rounds.

It's the morning after the fight before, and Our Enery enjoys breakfast with Albina while reading about his fifth-round British and Empire title victory over Welshman Dick Richardson at Wembley.

Jim 'The Bishop' Wicks looks on as Henry and Zora Folley weigh in for their second fight. In the background, left, film actor Stanley Baker, a long-time friend who followed Henry's career closely, and promoter Harry Levene. It was to end in tears, with a second-round knock-out defeat for Henry.

The most famous punch in British boxing history has landed, and Cassius Clay crashes against the ropes in the fourth round at Wembley Stadium in 1963. The 'Louisville Lip' was saved by the bell, and – with a little time-saving help of a torn glove – he came out for the fifth round to force a victory, when Henry suffered the unkindest cut of all.

Cassius Clay was now Muhammad Ali as he returned to London in 1966 to defend his world heavyweight title against Henry at Highbury Stadium in 1966. Viewsport showed the fight in cinemas across the nation, billing it as Britain's 'Fight of the Century'. Henry later became a popular television celebrity, starting his broadcasting career as a captain in the original *A Question of Sport*. Here he is (below) with question-master David Vine and Freddie Trueman, the cricketing legend who followed Cliff Morgan as his rival team captain.

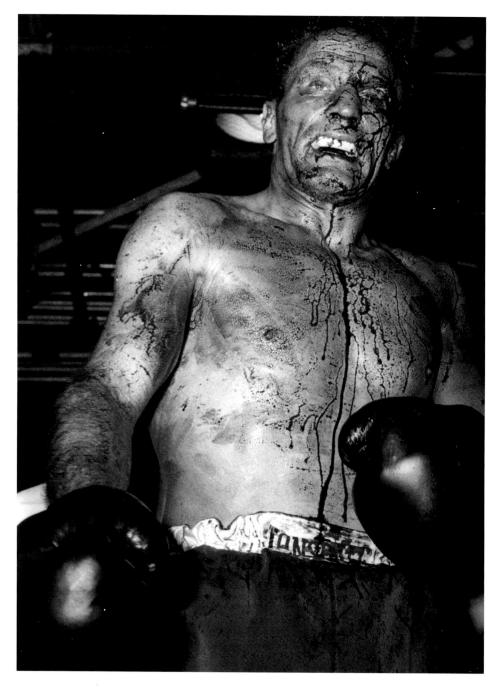

The end of a dream. Henry is covered in his own blood as his world-title challenge against Muhammad Ali is called off in the sixth round at Highbury in 1966.

same diligence and appetite he showed with a racecard in his hand, liked to go to a different restaurant every day, provided he could get on the blower to his bookmaker. 'Suddenly,' he said, 'I couldn't understand why Our Enery only wanted Italian food and kept insisting we go to Mario's. It took me a long time to twig he had fallen hook, line and sinker for Albina. When he told me he was going to marry her, I thought, "Blimey, I must make sure she don't feed him too much pasta."'

Actually, The Bishop was delighted and claimed matchmaking credit.

More of the great love story in the next chapter, but first back to the great glove story and the continuing saga of the serial with Joe Erskine. Their next battle was to produce one of the most dramatic finishes I ever saw to a fight anywhere in the world.

They breed 'em tough down at the Tiger Bay end of Cardiff and Joe was a tough Taff, all right. He was built like a Welsh back row forward yet was as light on his feet as a ballet dancer. He was as expressionless as the Sphinx. I hit him with some of the hardest punches I ever threw, but you would never know it from the look on his face. He was a cunning fox of a boxer who never showed emotions and he had more natural boxing skill than any British heavyweight I have seen before or since.

Our careers ran parallel like two express trains and every now and then we found ourselves on the same track. Our lines crossed for the first time in the semi-finals of the ABA light-heavyweight championship in 1952. It was the battle of the left jabs and I just managed to get the better of him over three evenly balanced rounds, which neutrals said presented traditional British boxing at its best.

We were both upright boxers who liked to move behind a stiff left jab and keep the action at long range. Where I always had the advantage over Joe was that I could hook off the jab, which meant I carried the heavier ammunition, but I have to own up to him being the cleverer boxer. He had such good rhythm and neat footwork that he could nullify the big punchers by keeping them off balance and out of distance; and he was a master at swaying and rolling on the ropes, letting opponents punch themselves out by hitting thin air. Believe me, that can be more tiring than hitting your target. Mind you, Joe's rope-a-dope tactics – long before Ali made them famous – were a dangerous practice that brought him a lot of trouble later in his career when the lead started to get into his legs.

Our styles didn't change very much from when we first fought, although I developed my punching power and stepped up my work rate to the body, whereas Joe stuck to his stylish jab-and-move tactics.

We met twice more as amateurs, both of them Army tournament contests, and we won one each on points. So when we turned pro in 1954, the score stood at two-one in my favour.

Our first fight with a purse rather than a tin pot at stake came at Harringay on 15 November 1955, in an official eliminator for the British championship. It was a repeat of our amateur contests, only this time spread over ten rounds, and it was Joe whose hand was raised by the referee at the end. I concentrated too much on conserving my energy in the early part of the fight and was unable to make up lost ground. I had Joe in trouble a couple of times with left hooks, but the wily bugger rolled, weaved and danced his way out of bother. I banged my left hand up on his tough old Welsh bonce in the seventh round, but no excuses, Joe deserved his win. That wasn't my night and as a superstitious sort I couldn't help reflecting on the fact that it was my thirteenth fight.

My fifth fight with Joe came in what I call my Black Year of 1957. I had been knocked out by a freak body blow from Joe Bygraves in a British Empire title fight in the February, then took the full ten-second count on my knees after Ingo's Bingo had landed on my jaw in a European title fight against Ingemar Johansson in the May. Then in the September I took on Erskine for the British title he had lifted off old war horse Johnny Williams.

My confidence wasn't exactly sky-high and again I made too cautious a start, allowing Joe to build an early lead. But I came back strongly and there were several times when even Joe's poker face couldn't hide the fact that I had hurt him. I was choked when the referee held up Joe's hand at the end of the fifteenth round because I thought I'd done just enough to have nicked the verdict.

Both Joe and I had managers who could claim the fastest tongue in the West. Joe was managed by a colourful Jewish Welshman called Benny Jacobs, like Jim Wicks a master at banging the publicity drum and with filling reporters' notebooks with outrageous, ticket-selling statements. When they were talking about having a smaller ring to suit me, he came up with the classic line: 'What an insult to Joe. You wouldn't show off a Goya in a brick outhouse.' Only he didn't say outhouse!

Because we left Jim and Benny to do much of the talking for us, the public got the impression there was bitterness and enmity between Joe and me. But that was all hocus-pocus created by our managers and the press. Outside the ring Joe and I were good pals, and inside the ropes we had total respect for each other.

Of our eight fights, the one I remember above all others is the sixth, when I at last proved beyond all argument that I was the guv'nor.

I was in the champion's corner for the fight, staged at London's Earls Court on 17 November 1959. Joe had lost his championship to

45

Brian London and I in turn had relieved London of both the British and Empire titles.

No denying that Erskine deserved the chance to try to regain the British crown, but he had never met me in more determined or confident mood. He weighed in at 13st 10lb, which gave him a four-pound weight advantage, but I was always happiest when boxing at 13st 6 or 7lb, and I felt superbly fit and raring to go.

I had made up my mind to try to hurt him early doors, rather than hang around, as in our previous professional contests. I was handicapped by a cut in the first round, but had the satisfaction of knowing I had really stunned him with a couple of meaty left hooks. In fact I had Joe grabbing hold of me while he cleared his head. He couldn't kid me with his poker face this time; I knew that I had hurt him.

There was a controversial finish to the end of the fifth round. Right through my career I specialised in throwing a hook off a jab, that is leading with the left and then all in the one movement throwing the same hand but this time from an angle. I had pierced Joe's guard with the jab and was into the reflex action of throwing the hook when the bell rang. Joe relaxed and my punch continued on its way and landed flush on his jaw.

Anybody who ever saw me box will confirm that I never once committed a deliberate foul in the ring. This was a complete accident, but Benny Jacobs didn't just make a meal of it but an entire banquet. He came diving into the ring and demanded that the Scottish referee Eugene Henderson should disqualify me. Mr Henderson was closer to the incident than anybody else apart from Joe and me, and he knew that the punch had started before the bell. He quite rightly ordered Benny back to his corner, but the volatile manager had made such a fuss that it planted the thought in some minds that I had gained an unfair advantage.

It was the first time in all my fights with Erskine when I felt in complete control despite the aggravation of the cut over my right eye. Joe was also cut, over his left eye, and as the fight moved into the last third I knew I'd got him going. He was breathing heavily, and his usually immaculate footwork had become plodding. At the end of each round I stared hard at my old mate, with my eyes saying, 'I'm coming to get you, Joe… I'm coming to get you…'

The end came in the twelfth round and it was one of the most frightening experiences I have ever known in the ring. Joe was doing one of his rolling and weaving acts on the ropes, but he was tired and lacked his usual split-second timing. I caught him with a cracker of a left hook to the jaw and he slid down the ropes for the first count either of us had ever taken in our six meetings. He was unwisely – and unsteadily – up at seven and I quickly moved in with a two-fisted attack that sent him down for another seven count.

I wish referee Henderson had moved in because Joe was in no position to defend himself, but I was waved forward and this time I let fly with a left-right combination followed by a left hook that carried every ounce of my strength. Poor Joe went flying backwards, the top half of his body crashing under the middle rope. He was arched over the bottom rope like a giant violin bow, and he was out to the world. The referee wisely didn't bother to count but stopped the fight there and then, waving for assistance to get the unconscious Joe disentangled from the ropes.

Even in this sweet moment of victory I felt sick because I thought Joe had broken his back. Jim Wicks felt the same, and when I returned to the corner he was visibly shivering with fright and shock.

Thank God, Joe recovered after some treatment from the ringside doctor and suffered only bruising to his back. It could have been so much worse.

Like I say, for all our rivalry Joe and I were good buddies and the last thing I wanted was to see him seriously injured. Boxing is a hard, hard sport, but you'd be surprised how close and caring opponents become once the punching is over.

Crafty old Benny Jacobs, who somehow kept on managing Joe after he had been accused of gambling away his purse money, made the most of the punch that I landed as the bell rang in the fifth round. He kicked up such a stink that we had to give Joe another crack at the title. We fought at Wembley on 21 March 1961 and it lasted only fifteen minutes. My left hand was never out of his face and both of his eyes were cut and closing when his corner took the referee's advice and retired him at the end of the fifth round. It was a memorable moment for me because this third successful championship defence won me my first Lonsdale Belt outright. For me, the Lonsdale Belt – named after one of the original father figures of boxing and awarded to winners of British title fights – was the premier prize in the sport, and to win one outright was a dream come true. Little did I know that I would get another two in my trophy cabinet before I packed it in. That would have sounded too far-fetched.

Just over a year later, Joe and I were at it again, this time in Manchester, and again my British and Empire titles were at stake. He was past his best and very puffy around the eyes, and he lacked the mobility that had made him such a difficult target in his prime.

I concentrated on shovelling as many lefts as I could through his defence as in the previous fight, and I closed one of his eyes and gashed the other before the referee sensibly stopped the one-way traffic in the ninth round.

It was our eighth and last fight, so I finished 5–3 ahead in our series that spanned the best ten years of our fighting lives. But neither of us was ever really a loser because we won each other's friendship and respect.

Joe battled on for a couple of years after our final fight but was never the same major force in the game and he retired in 1964 after a points defeat by Billy Walker, an all-heart fighter who would have struggled to lay a glove on him in his majestic prime.

Joe, who sadly passed on in 1990 aged just fifty-six, turned professional at the same time as Henry in 1954. While he retired ten years later, amazingly Henry boxed on for another seven years... as a happily married man.

ROUND 5

MARRIAGE, TAX AND CAULIFLOWERS

Henry did not just embrace Albina, but her entire Italian culture and also her religion. He converted to Roman Catholicism from non-practising Church of England and became a devout follower who never publicly pushed or promoted his new beliefs but was very happy to talk about them to anybody who was interested.

All those of us who knew Henry well were aware how his marriage in January 1960 changed him into a more confident, well-rounded person, whose love for Albina almost shone out of him. Suddenly, from living a rather sheltered existence that allowed little room outside the narrow village world of boxing-boxing-boxing, he quickly established himself as a contented family man. With the arrival of his adored sons, Henry Marco and John Pietro, he was the epitome of a proud, doting dad and he settled down to what was to become forty-seven years of married bliss – what all close observers will confirm was the near-perfect marriage. It was a match made in heaven and in their company you could not but help being intoxicated by their love and affection.

They looked the odd couple, Henry standing a fraction under 6ft 2in, Albina not much above five feet in her high heels; but she always gave as good as she got in mock arguments. Whenever her mother was over from Italy she used to tell Albina off for not waiting on her husband hand and foot, which was the accepted way in the peasant world from which she came. Albina used to tell anybody in listening distance: 'If he thinks I'm his servant, he is in for a disappointment.' Henry would just give a big grin and a shrug, and say: 'Make us a cup of tea, love!'

Albina took over Henry's diary, later with the dedicated help of highly respected showbusiness and sports agent and family friend, Patsy Martin – a full-time job if ever there was one, because he was always in demand for charity events and he very rarely said no. If anybody ever earned his popularity by putting something back into the community it was Our Enery. He was a true man of the people, never asking for a penny piece in return for his time and happy to help out any deserving cause.

There are several boxing writers who walked around padded with extra pounds because of the amazing hospitality shown them by Albina. The morning after any one of Henry's fights – win or lose – she would cook breakfasts for the story-seeking evening newspaper reporters and photographers, who dropped into their pleasant three-bedroom house within sight and sound of Wembley Stadium.

Then the daily newspaper boys arrived in the early afternoon and Albina would insist on cooking them lunch, or at the very least making them a snack meal. It was as if she thought she was still work-ing in the restaurant.

We talked boxing during all these meals and the only person who did not understand what we were on about was Albina. She quietly detested the sport and thought it was barbaric. Only once did she ever attend a fight night, when Henry challenged Ali for the world title. She spent the six rounds with the fight programme covering her face and sick to the stomach with nerves. 'Henry knows how I feel about boxing,' she told me. 'But I wouldn't dream of mentioning that I'd like him to retire; that has to be his decision. It would be out of order for me to even bring the subject up. I knew what he did and the dangers he faced when I married him, and I just make sure I'm always there for him when he comes home with his bruises and cut eyes. I feel his pain, but it's his job and it's not for me to interfere. We have complete faith in Mr Wicks to always make the right decisions. I would hate it if our sons wanted to box, but I wouldn't stop them. Men must do what men must do, but I will be very relieved and happy when Henry does decide to hang up his gloves and lead a normal life.'

Henry was besotted with Albina in what was very much a two-way love affair.

I was the luckiest man in the world to find Albina. She had been under my nose for years without me realising the chemistry between us. She used to serve Jim and me at Mario's from when she was sixteen, but it was all of five years before I thought to myself, 'Aye aye, she's a bit special.'

I was not exactly a Casanova type and I clumsily started flirting with her. She was used to that sort of thing with customers and just took it as banter. I asked her out to the pictures one night and said I would collect her on the Saturday. She agreed, thinking that I was joking. But when I called into the restaurant to pick her up, she was in uniform and working. She had not taken me seriously and I don't know who was more embarrassed when she realised I meant it. Anyway, we eventually got our wires uncrossed and – I don't want this to sound too soppy – we just fell head over heels for each other.

It was the best thing that ever happened to me. She has become not only my wife but my best friend and also organiser. Albina knows nothing about boxing, which is a good thing because it means I have something else to talk about when I get home rather than who was doing what in the fight game. People often comment that I am always immaculately booted and suited, and that's the Albina influence. She has that natural Italian taste for all things elegant and stylish, and makes sure I am clothed just right for whatever charity or commercial job I'm doing or appearance I'm making.

She has given me two wonderful sons and introduced me to the Italian family way of life. I'm very proud of our boys, Henry Marco and John Pietro, and they could not have a better mother. Thanks to Albina, I've discovered the contentment and fulfilment that the Roman Catholic religion can bring. I am the last person to try to push my newfound beliefs down other people's throats, but all I know is it's made me a better person and our family is built on a rock-solid foundation of love and faith.

She was just the breath of fresh air I needed. I am a very lucky man.

Helped by brother George, Henry put his plastering and building experience to work and gradually extended the Wembley house to a five-bedroom luxury home, with a huge new lounge and an extra bathroom. George even moved in with them until his marriage to his boss's daughter, Barbara Reynolds.

Those were the days when tax took a huge bite out of earnings and Henry found himself paying 16s 9d from every pound to the taxman. In modern parlance, he was left with just over 20p from each pound that he earned. Jim Wicks once showed me Henry's tax slip: 'Earnings for the year £36,000, tax bill £29,000'. This was why he rationed his ring appearances to two or three a year. For several years,

Jim and Henry – supported by Scottish MP Tam Dalyell – fought to have sportsmen's earnings assessed over a full year as with writers and artists, but that was one contest where they were always outpointed by the taxman. 'We never dodged tax in our lives,' said Jim Wicks. 'But it is a system that makes people become fiddlers like that Yehudi wossisname.'

To supplement his earnings from boxing, Henry later went into partnership in a greengrocery shop in Wembley. For once he cocked a deaf 'un to advice from Jim Wicks, who told him: 'What d'you know about spuds or how long it takes for fruit to rot? You're making a mistake, Enery. You've gone bananas.'

Within three years Henry had lost what was then the huge amount of more than £10,000 on the business and he put up the shutters on the shop, paid off outstanding bills and concentrated full time on the thing he did best, boxing. It had been more painful than cauliflower ears.

That was a very stressful time in our lives. On the surface it looked to outsiders as if the Coopers were doing well. A successful boxing career and a thriving greengrocery shop in Wembley High Street. In truth, the taxman was taking a massive bite of my boxing earnings and the greengrocer's was a disaster.

I went into it on the spur of the moment with a bloke I met on holiday in Las Palmas, who happened to be called Harry Cooper but was no relation. We got friendly and he told me he had a greengrocer's stall in Holloway and was thinking of opening a shop in Wembley. One thing led to another and I suddenly got caught up by his enthusiasm and lobbed some money into the project and became a partner. The shop was in my name, so I got all the publicity – and all the flak from suppliers wanting payment when things went, excuse the pun, pear shaped. It was bloody 'orrible to go into the shop and have some old dear coming up to you and saying, "Ere, Enery, those plums I bought here last week were hard and very sharp...' I went into the business blind and came out nearly broke. As fast as I was earning in the ring my money was being drained by the shop. I started out as a sleeping partner, calling in a couple of times a week, but then found it was taking up four and five days as I tried to turn it around. You could say I paid for the mistake but learned from the experience. In future, I decided I would only put my money into things I understood.

Sadly, as we will learn later, Henry did not listen to his own advice.

The Bishop was concerned that married life was in danger of making Henry soft and he used to insist on him leaving home for five weeks before each fight to 'get mean and lean.' The boxing axiom has always been that home comforts breed soft fighters, all the way back to legends of the ring like Jack Dempsey and Joe Louis. They always went away to training camps to escape temptations and distractions. Fighters need to be single-minded and being pampered at home is known to take the edge off, particularly when the relaxation includes sexual diversions.

By the time Henry was under orders to train away from home, I was writing a column for *Boxing News* called 'Around the Gyms with Ross Martin'. Editor Tim Riley gave me my *nom de plume*, inspired by a case of Martini Rossi under his desk. I became a regular at Henry's training sessions, watching him go through a regimented routine that for championship fights included daily sparring sessions against a parade of partners under instruction to adopt set styles. They got paid anything from £20 to £100 a round, depending on the size of Henry's purse. His specially manufactured headguard had leather flaps to protect his vulnerable eyebrows.

Nice guy Henry was mean in the gym and showed his sparring partners no mercy, while wearing well-padded 16-ounce gloves that protected his hands – and also saved his hired 'opponents' from serious damage. When fighting he would wear six-ounce, later eight-ounce gloves, and before every fight or sparring session he would spend thirty minutes carefully bandaging his hands. 'I rarely take it easy against sparring partners,' he told me. 'That can breed bad habits, which you can take into the ring with you for the proper fight. We rarely get sparring partners volunteering to come back. They are well paid, but have to earn their corn.'

Once Henry had established himself as a champion, he trained mainly at the Bull's Head gymnasium in Chislehurst, briefly at the Fellowship Inn on the Bellingham Estate, then at the Clive Hotel in Hampstead and the Noble Art gym on Haverstock Hill. But none of them had the same spit-and-sawdust atmosphere of his original head-quarters at the Thomas a Becket, where the nostrils were assaulted by the odour of embrocation, liniment, cigars and stale sweat mixed with the pungent aroma from the beer cellars, while the thud-thud-thud of the heavy bags and the rhythmic staccato of the skipping ropes provided a rich symphony of sound. The Cooper twins prided themselves on their pace and grace on the skipping ropes and used to compete with each other to see who could produce the fastest combi-nation punches on the speedball. Spectators at the Thomas a Becket would often break into applause when watching the twins skipping in unison and the blur of fists as Henry and George punished the punchbag and speedball.

I used to walk across Tower Bridge from my Cable Street home to the Becket in Old Kent Road, stopping en route for a slurp of tea on the Bridge with my policeman brother, George, the black sheep of our family, who was on security duty on the Bridge and had a sentry box with a Thermos flask tucked out of sight.

When I told The Bishop that my brother was a City policeman who guarded Tower Bridge, he announced to the gym: 'Careful what you say, we've got an Old Bill snout in our midst. He's a regular Miss Marble.'

I was a real mug for Jim's leg-pulling stories and he once almost had me printing a piece in my gossip column that he was going to give all his boxers the sort of controversial monkey gland injections that the Wolves players had had before the 1939 FA Cup final. As I took down copious notes, Henry whispered: 'Jim's making a right monkey out of you, Norm.'

The Bishop was an affable, jovial man, but rival promoters Jack Solomons and Harry Levene both found him a Rottweiler when it came to negotiating. His one objective was to get the best possible deal for his boxers. Levene, himself a mean miserly man when negotiating (as I often discovered to my cost when asking for my wages as PR for his boxing shows), once told me: 'That scoundrel Jim Wicks should wear a mask and carry a gun the way he bargains for his boxers. He gets away with robbery.'

During purse negotiations, Solomons used to yell at him: 'I thought we were supposed to be friends.' Jim, holding all the cards, would reply: 'This isn't about friendship, this is about business and I'm here representing my boy.'

That neatly tees up a true story that entrepreneur Jarvis Astaire told Henry and me during a charity dinner at the London Hilton: 'Elvis was at his peak and had never performed in Europe. I was determined to bring him to Britain and I phoned his manager, the notorious "Colonel" Tom Parker. I offered him £2 million for Elvis to perform in London. That was an astronomical amount at the time.

The Colonel pondered for a while, and then replied: "That's a very generous offer. Now, what about the boy…?"'"

I think it fair to say that Jarvis was all shook up.

Our hero Henry must have been one of the best-fed boxers in history. As well as the dishes beautifully prepared by Albina, when he was not in training The Bishop would take him every week to Simpson's in The Strand on Mondays, where they were famous for their roast beef, Peter Mario's on the Wednesday for their Italian cuisine, and always fish on Fridays at Manzi's in Leicester Square or Sheekey's just off Charing Cross Road. They were the 'in' places to be seen and Jim was always keen for Henry to keep a high profile. 'It's all about putting bums on seats,' he explained. 'The more people see Enery around, the more they'll want to come and see him box.'

Henry had one fight in 1960 that failed to get into the record books. Perhaps 'fight' is a bit of an exaggeration, because there was only one blow thrown. Driving home from a lunch celebrating the twins' twenty-sixth birthday on 3 May, Henry inadvertently cut up a cyclist after overtaking him. As he pulled into the kerb, the cyclist deliberately rode his bike into Henry's car and bashed on the side. Henry wound down the driver's side window to ask what was occurring and the man – middle-aged, no more than 5ft 5in tall and a bantamweight – leaned in towards him and cracked him on the nose with a back hander. Henry, George and Jim Wicks immediately climbed out of the car, surrounding the assailant. 'You cheeky little so-and-so,' Henry said, or words to that effect. The diminutive cyclist looked up into Henry's face and said: 'You feel brave 'cos there's three of you…' The twins and Jim Wicks collapsed laughing and the aggrieved man, not seeing the funny side, got on his bike and rode off, muttering to himself.

Now back to the *real* boxing. After a ten-month lay-off that included a honeymoon in Italy, Henry had his first fight as a married man against the high-ranking Roy Harris at Wembley Pool on 13 September 1960. Born in the town of Cut 'n' Shoot, Texas, Harris had gone twelve rounds in a world championship challenge against Floyd Patterson in August 1958 before his corner threw in the towel.

Harris had clearly been warned about Our Enery's left hook and spent almost the entire fight backing off to his left as Henry jabbed his way to a comfortable ten rounds points victory. In the build-up to the contest, the Texan talked like a man who had swallowed a dictionary and it was no surprise when upon retiring from the ring he became a lawyer. 'He had a brain like wossaname, Adolf Einstein,' said The Bishop. 'But he was a pretty dumb fighter.'

Next up on 6 December 1960 was the hefty Argentine Alex Miteff, who had pulled out of the fight with injury when Zora Folley substituted. Henry was completely in command but got careless in the tenth and last round and walked into a swinging right hand, taking a nine count. 'That last round wasn't good for the old ticker,' said white-as-a-sheet Jim Wicks. 'I almost had a cardigan arrest.' Henry dedicated his points victory to his newborn son Henry Marco.

On 21 March 1961, Henry won his first Lonsdale Belt outright when he stopped a completely outgunned Joe Erskine in five rounds at Wembley, and the air was now thick with talk of a world title challenge against Floyd Patterson after his three-fight saga with Ingemar Johansson. The Bishop had direct talks with Floyd's manager Cus D'Amato, but put them on hold when Henry's left shoulder started to give painful problems. He went to leading orthopaedic surgeon Bill Tucker for treatment and was told that his left arm, gnarled left hand and shoulder – overworked in plastering and boxing – were as worn as those of a sixty-year-old man.

Meantime Sonny Liston took over the world title assignment and blasted Patterson to defeat in one round. 'Told you he was a bloody animal,' said The Bishop.

Following a nine-month rest after his latest demolition of Erskine, Henry took a rematch with Zora Folley and for once in his life failed to prepare properly for a fight. He talked Jim Wicks into letting him stay at home, going to the gym daily for his sparring and then returning to Albina's loving arms. Instead of the mean lean fighting machine, he became a big softie and was far too relaxed as he climbed into the Wembley Pool ring on 5 December 1961 to take on one of the classiest box-fighters never to win a world title. He paid the price for his rare lack of professionalism when Folley fired in a short right to the jaw in the second round that knocked him spark out. When his senses cleared, he agreed with his manager's collective decision: 'We will never train at home again.'

It was important for Henry to get his confidence back as quickly as possible and five weeks later they brought over another Texan in the bulky shape of Tony Hughes, whose main claim to fame was that he was the protégé of ring legend Rocky Marciano. Hughes was not nearly as formidable as his master and the Rock pulled him out of the fight after Henry had pummelled him for five rounds.

We were more interested in meeting and talking to Rocky than his young prospect. He had been one of our heroes when we were kids and he won the world championship the year we retained the ABA light-heavyweight title.

What a shock we got when we met him at the pre-fight press conference. We expected some sort of a monster, but he was quietly spoken, very modest and a proper gentleman. It was the complete opposite to the way he was in the ring, when he resorted to the rules of the jungle. I'll never forget the brutal way he beat our local hero Don Cockell in a world title fight in San Francisco. He did everything but hit him with the corner stool. He committed so many fouls that if it had been fought in Britain he would have been slung out after a minute. I would have hated to fight him. He was always all over his opponents, bashing them with his elbows, head and a right hand that could have sunk a battleship.

I don't mind admitting that I cried the day he was killed in an air crash the day before his forty-sixth birthday. His real name was Rocco Marchegiano and he was idolised by all Italians. Shortly before he died he featured in a computerised fight with Muhammad Ali, and they released a film showing Rocky stopping Ali late in the fight. Years later, Ali told me that they had filmed three endings: one with Rocky winning, another with Ali winning and a fifteen-round draw. It was better box office to release the version with Rocky winning. Ali, of course, had an opinion on that, 'Couldn't have a black man –' he used the N word '– beating the greatest white heavyweight in history.'

Fast forward to 1987 and a series I created for ITV called *Who's the Greatest?* We matched Ali against Rocky, with a jury of twelve members of the public listening to the arguments put by Eamonn Andrews for Rocky and, for Ali, actor Dennis Waterman, whose brother Peter was an exceptional British and European welterweight champion. Eamonn called Henry as his witness, and Waterman summoned Brian London. My dear pal Brian Moore was the judge.

After listening to each case and watching videos of the action, the jury voted 9–3 for Ali.

In the dressing-room afterwards a shaking, perspiring and clearly unwell Eamonn and Henry both agreed they did well to get three members of the jury to vote for Rocky. 'No question Ali was the greatest,' said Henry. 'I guess I have just perjured myself.'

It was Eamonn's final television appearance and following his passing a few weeks later Henry assisted in the rites of Communion at the thanksgiving mass for our old friend at Westminster Cathedral. I was a member of Eamonn's *This Is Your Life* scriptwriting team and can vouch that he was the most conscientious and masterful broadcaster in the television business, like Henry a professional from tip to toe. I know Henry would want me to pay Eamonn his dues in this book as being one of the friendliest and finest men you could ever wish to meet.

Henry's next re-establishing fight was against experienced black American Wayne Bethea at the vast Belle Vue Stadium in Manchester on 26 February 1962. It was an excellent workout for our hero and he won comfortably on points over ten rounds before, two months later, stopping a worn-out Joe Erskine in nine rounds at Nottingham. For poor old Joe, it was downhill to retirement, while for Henry big plans were being hatched.

He stopped Dick Richardson again in the fifth round with a barrage of left hooks at Wembley on 26 March 1963, retaining his British and Empire titles. For one of the few times in his career, Henry lost his temper in the ring when the bulldozing Richardson caught him with a punch after the bell to end the third round. He retaliated with a combination of punches that rocked the huge Welshman and they had to be pulled apart by the referee and cornermen. 'We were very annoyed with Our Enery,' said a poker-faced Jim Wicks. 'We don't get paid for fighting between rounds and we could have got ourselves disqualified. That would have been a catastrophe.' The press boys looked at him amazed. He actually did mean 'a catastrophe'.

Jim knew that negotiations were close to being completed for a world title fight eliminator – against a young American upstart from Louisville, Kentucky, by the name of Cassius Marcellus Clay.

ROUND 6

ENERY'S 'AMMER AND THE FEAT OF CLAY

An unfunny thing happened to Cassius Clay on his way to a world championship challenge against Sonny Liston. Henry whacked him on the whiskers with his famed and feared left hook and for a few dramatic moments it looked as if he had thrown a spanner – or, rather, a hammer – into the works.

Before telling Henry's inside story of his most famous fight, let's first of all sort out the source of the nickname for 'Enery's 'Ammer'. Even Henry used to get it wrong, telling interviewers that it had been dreamt up by 'either Walter Bartleman in the *Evening Star*, Des Hackett in *The Express* or Peter Wilson in *The Mirror*.'

It came in fact from the mouth of Jim Wicks and was captured and cemented by the pencil of *Daily Express* sports cartoonist Roy Ullyett, who with celebrated columnist Desmond Hackett often used to join Henry and The Bishop for their Friday fish lunches in Soho. I was a teammate of theirs for ten years in my earlier life as chief football reporter for *The Express* and I ghosted Roy's *While I Still Have Lead In My Pencil* autobiography, in which he revealed: 'Jim Wicks used to talk about "Our Enery's 'Ammer" during our lunches and one day

I felt inspired to go back to the office and draw a cartoon of Henry with a hammer in his left hand. From then on everybody called the left hook Enery's 'Ammer. I never did collect my royalties.'

When Henry came to Roy's funeral some years later, I gave the eulogy and told the story of how, when Henry had a knee operation, he drew a cartoon showing the surgeon – scalpel in hand – standing over the anesthetised Henry as a nurse says: 'This is one heck of a time to ask, "Does Henry have a good left hook and a bad right knee, or a good left knee and a bad right hook?"'

Henry told me after the service: 'I roared with laughter at the memory of that cartoon. It was a classic. I hope Roy's family don't think I was being disrespectful.' Roy, the man who immortalised 'Enery's 'Ammer', would have taken it as the best compliment he could have had.

The most talked-about delivery of the 'Ammer came in the last seconds of the fourth round of a scheduled ten rounder at Wembley Stadium on 18 June 1963. On the receiving end: the most talked-about and talkative heavyweight in history, Cassius Clay. Years later, Henry recalled for me the unforgettable events leading up to a fight that was an official eliminator for the world title held by the fearsome Sonny Liston:

From the moment the match was made we fancied our chances of catching Clay with the left hook. He had a hands-down style of boxing that left his chin unguarded, and throughout our training for the fight we practised feinting with our right and then whipping over the left hook.

We got our sparring partners to skip backwards Clay-style with their hands down, and we got into the habit of moving diagonally forward so as to crowd Clay on to the ropes where he could not use his foot speed to get out of trouble.

Jim Wicks asked his American contacts whose style most resembled Clay's and he was told that a Mississippi-born heavyweight called Alonzo Johnson could do a perfect imitation. We brought him in as my chief sparring partner and he did a great job for us, boxing in Ali's hands-down, fast-moving style. Alonzo was a lovely feller who just got on with his job, taking a lot of stick without complaint. He had boxed Clay in his eighth fight and lost on points over ten rounds. 'I done got robbed,' he told us. 'I fought in Clay's hometown of Louisville and even his own fans booed the verdict.' It was the first of Ali's fights to be shown on national television and he got a roasting from the critics. Several of them agreed that Alonzo should have got at least a draw.

We'd been more aware than most of the style of Clay for three years. We had watched on telly when he outpointed one of our old opponents, the Aussie Tony Madigan, in the Olympic light-heavyweight semi-finals in Rome in 1960. Our opinion then was that he was flash, too fast on his feet to be a big hitter and that his chin was always a tempting target. We reckoned he had taken a lot of his amateurish habits into the professional game with him and saw flaws in his defence that we were determined to expose.

The British public didn't like Clay at all when he arrived in London for the fight, shooting his mouth off and shouting things like, 'Any more jive, and Cooper will fall in five.' And he went way too far when he called me a bum and a cripple. I never found the need to insult my opponents and saying things like that was disrespectful and unnecessary. People thought he was getting under our skin because we refused to react to his taunts, but we were happy for him to fill pages and pages with his rabbiting because we were on a percentage of ancillary rights and so the more people who watched on TV or at the cinema, the more dosh we got.

Clay didn't do himself any favours with the crowd when he came swaggering into the ring wearing a huge crown that somebody had found for him in the wardrobes at the Palladium, where we weighed in with 2,000 people looking on from the theatre seats. He wore the pantomime crown for a laugh but most spectators thought it was in poor taste and booed him into the ring. I just watched it all with a sort of tight smile and thought what a nutter he was.

The only upmanship I got on him was when we were posing for photographs at the weigh-in and I noticed he had just one hair growing from his chest. I reached forward and pulled it out, and his eyes opened wide before he laughed out loud.

We pulled a stroke at the weigh-in. Jim was concerned that me weighing just under thirteen stone would give Clay a psychological boost. I had worked so hard in training that I was barely over the light-heavyweight limit. Jim, of course, was an expert on handicaps and racing weights, and he arranged for me to step on the scales with flat lead plate-weights in the sole of my boxing boots and I held another lead weight in my right hand. They added about six pounds. Not a lot, but it at least made me seem like a heavyweight. What a rascal Jim could be!

It was an unforgettable big fight night, full of pomp and ceremony as Jack Solomons called on every trick he had learned in his long career as a promoter who always mixed showbiz with boxing. To call the atmosphere electric would have been an understatement; more like nuclear. Liz Taylor and Richard Burton, the world's most glamorous couple at the time and fresh from making the controversial *Cleopatra*, were among the 55,000-strong crowd singing in drizzling rain to the music of the Coldstream Guards band. Then, heralded by eight trumpeters dressed as if for a coronation, came the two gladiators, picked out in spotlights, Henry from the home dressing-room used by England's footballers and Clay approaching from where the visiting teams prepared for action. Ear-splitting cheers for Cooper, just as loud jeers for the cocky Clay, who looked more clown than king with the Palladium pantomime crown perched on his head. The choruses of derision when Clay climbed into the ring were so loud that the ring announcements could hardly be heard. It was sheer bedlam. But all the hullabaloo had no effect on the kid from Kentucky as he strutted around the ring as if he owned Wembley.

Henry, eight years older and twenty-six pounds lighter than his jet-paced opponent, surprised Clay by opening up much more aggressively than in his usual cautious starts to contests, and within a minute referee Tommy Little was warning Clay for holding as Henry worked to the body like a man possessed. 'Gaseous Cassius' suddenly knew it was not going to be as easy as he had been boasting and he twice looked appealingly at the referee as Henry roughed him up inside, trying to make the most of his experience as a professional against a relative baby having only his nineteenth fight.

At the end of a fast and furious first round there was a sign of blood – and it was coming from Clay's nose, on which the Cooper jab had been beating a tattoo.

The second round was even, with Clay now carrying the fight to Cooper and jabbing more effectively. Henry tried hard to drive him back to the ropes, but he was dancing and side-stepping his way out of danger every time the British champion set himself for a two-fisted attack. He was responding to the shouted commands from trainer Angelo Dundee: 'Stick and move… stick and move…' In English lingo, that meant jab and move.

All was going to plan for Henry until in the third round he was hit by his old hoodoo – Clay had opened a cut over his left eye with a chopping right hand counter. Suddenly Henry was looking through a veil of blood and now there was desperation in his punches as Clay began toying with him so contemptuously that Bill Faversham – head of the syndicate of white businessmen who owned his contract – screamed out: 'Stop clowning, Clay, and get the job done!' He knew that a multi-million dollar title fight with Liston was next on the menu and Sonny's manager Jack Nilon was there to confirm it.

Jim Wicks wanted to stop the fight at the end of the third round because the gash was so deep, but Henry demanded one more round. And what a round!

It has become etched into fight folklore, with blurred and exaggerated details. But from this distance, let's try to get the facts right and sort the truth from the legend.

Clay continued to clown and box with his hands down at his waist, rolling out of the way of Henry's punches and making him miss with clever and at times audacious ring movement. It was clear – cockily and confidently – he was trying to make the fight last until the fifth round, as he had so noisily predicted. Syndicate boss Faversham was going apoplectic because he knew the millions of dollars that were riding on a victory.

Clay could not have cared less about Faversham and his business partners, against whom he was secretly plotting, ready for a change of name and management. He was interested only in getting the nominated round right, as he had done in most of his previous fights. It was a dangerous gimmick, an ego trip through a minefield. While he was playing the fool it meant he was not hitting Henry and making the cut worse, and all the time our hero was plotting and planning how he could get home with his hammer.

The round was into its last ten seconds when Clay got himself trapped in a neutral corner as Henry fired a succession of left jabs. They were all range finders for the following left hook that landed on an arc flush on the right side of Clay's jaw.

He fell back into the ropes and slithered slowly to the canvas like a giant puppet that had suddenly had its strings cut away. His eyes were

as wide as if he had been hypnotised, mirroring a mixture of astonish-
ment and anguish. The count had reached five and Clay (dropped
only once before, by Sonny Banks) made the novice decision to get
up on legs that were betraying him, but before Henry – acknowledged
as one of the best finishers in the business – could move in, the bell
rang. Never before in the history of British sport had the ringing of a
bell stopped the nation's breath.

There was pandemonium and those of us used to being at
Wembley for FA Cup finals and England football internationals were
convinced we had never heard a roar like the one that greeted Clay's
knockdown. It was not so much like a clap of thunder as an animal
growl coming from thousands of British throats. This was Last Night
of the Proms xenophobia but with a savagery that would have rocked
the bust of Henry Wood off its plinth. Richard Burton's famous Welsh
voice could be heard booming: 'Finish him, Henry, finish him!' Liz
Taylor was hiding her face.

Clay tried to show he was unhurt, but his senses were so scattered
that he reeled back to his corner like a drunk on his way home from
the pub. Angelo Dundee slapped his thighs as he sat him down
on the stool and as sponged water rained on Clay's head he instinc-
tively tried to stand up as if to get back into the fight. What appeared to
be illegal smelling salts were pressed under his nostrils and he pulled
a grotesque face that made him look much older than his twenty-one
years. While all this was going on, the crafty, ring-wise Dundee was
summoning referee Tommy Little to show him that there was a split
in Ali's right glove – not confessing until years later that he had made
the split worse by digging in his thumb and pushing out horsehair.

Now we enter the world of myth and mystery. Many observers,
including experienced boxing writers, claimed that Dundee's chicanery earned Clay an extra twenty to thirty seconds of recovery time.

Even Henry, deluded by the reports, used to repeat the allegation in his after-dinner speeches.

Much as I would like to perpetuate the legend, I have to say I have been in the BBC archives department and watched the unedited version of the fight in real time. The interval between the fourth and fifth rounds actually lasted sixty-six seconds, which means that the Dundee gamesmanship gained just an extra six seconds. Some reports even said that Clay had his glove changed; I can state categorically that when Clay went out for the fifth round the new glove had not even arrived at ringside. My dad was a boxing fanatic who worked as gloves-minder for Jack Solomons in return for a free ticket to the major fights. His acquaintance with the veteran promoter went back to pre-war days, when Jack was in the fishmongering and betting business and Dad the bookie's runner.

Dad told me: 'The box in which the spare set of gloves was kept was never out of my sight and the British Boxing Board of Control steward didn't ask for the replacement glove until the fifth round was under way.'

By the time the glove was relayed to the ringside, the fight was all over. Clay came out for the fifth round with the one intention of getting things finished before Henry could give him another taste of his hammer. A fusillade of lefts and rights landed on his damaged eye and blood gushed as if being pumped out.

Liz Taylor, now brave enough to watch, was among the many ringside spectators screaming for referee Tommy Little to stop the fight. It was not a pretty sight.

After one minute fifteen seconds of the fifth round, and with a desperate Jim Wicks up on the apron of the ring ready to throw in the towel, the referee waved his arms and called it off, saying to our bloody hero: 'Sorry, chum, the fight's over.'

Henry, hitting the air in frustration, said: 'We didn't do bad for a bum and a cripple, did we?'

The Bishop said: 'Enery did us proud, but the mince pie let us down.' Malapropism gave way to Cockney rhyming slang, a language in which Wicks was fluent.

Clay, to his credit, was polite and dignified in victory, refusing to put the crown back on as one of his entourage jumped into the ring with it. He said many times later: 'Henry hit me so hard he shook up my ancestors in Africa.'

Henry had almost buttoned the Louisville Lip and the fact that he was knocked down sent signals to the Liston camp that he would be easy meat for old Sonny. The crown passed to Clay when he humiliated Liston in two fights, during which Cassius made his break with the all-white syndicate which he claimed owned him like a slave, changed his name to Muhammad Ali and became the puppet of Black Muslims. He was never really his own man during his boxing career.

Even in defeat, Henry was a hero and the fight made him famous around the world. But for the rest of his life he had to live with the 'if only' scenario.

If only we had landed the left hook in the first minute of the round rather than the last we're convinced we would have knocked him out. We don't like blowing our own trumpet, but there were few who could match us for finishing off an opponent if we had him going... and Clay was out on his feet when he scrambled up. That showed his inexperience and also that he didn't know what day it was. Those big eyes of his were rolling and his legs were wobbly like jelly.

He should have been looking to stay down for at least eight seconds. We know we'd have finished him off if the bell had not rung. He was also lucky to fall against the ropes. If I'd landed the punch when we were in the centre of the ring I don't think he would have got up in twenty seconds, let alone ten.

Ali, as he became, often said that the sight of blood sickened him and that he wanted to look away when I was bleeding. He probably meant that in the cold light of day, but in the ring when it mattered he saw his advantage and came after me with an animal instinct for a finish. I was the prey and he was the hunter, and he wasn't going to let me go. And I don't blame him. The old fight game ain't for faint hearts.

I would have done exactly the same thing in his boots. There were no bad feelings between us after it was all over. I knew he didn't mean half the things he said during the build-up to the fight. He was a master showman, and did his job in getting bums on seats. To be honest, I really liked the bloke and always found him amusing company. He called himself The Greatest, and for many people he was, but I think Joe Louis was probably the best heavyweight of them all. Clay or Ali, or whatever you want to call him, was certainly the greatest entertainer.

Thirteen years after the Cooper-Clay fight I spent three weeks with the by then Muhammad Ali, working as a publicist on his world title defence against Yorkshire lionheart Richard Dunn in Munich. He was a real charmer away from the microphones and cameras, talking not much above a whisper in head-to-head conversation as he gave me his view of the first fight with Henry:

I'd never been hit as hard as Henry hit me that night. Man, it really did shake up my ancestors in Africa. When I got up I didn't know whether I was in London or Louisville, but I was a young man and had good recovery powers. I knew exactly what I had to do and went out and finished him in the fifth, just the way I'd planned. Jack Nilon, Liston's manager, was at the ringside and that knockdown convinced him I'd be eaten by Old Sonny. B-i-g mistake! What it proved is that I could take a punch, because that would have finished off most opponents. Henry is a proper English gent and took his defeat like the true sportsman he is. I apologised for calling him a cripple and a bum. He knew I was just trying to sell tickets and it worked because that great stadium at Wembley was packed. Ninety-nine per cent of the crowd were rooting for Henry and wanted to see my big mouth shut. That made me all the more determined to win in style in the fifth, but the knockdown took the shine off my win. If Henry had not been a bleeder he might have done even better in his career, but he was champion of Britain, the Commonwealth and the whole of Europe, so I guess that was not bad. But I became champion of the w-h-o-l-e world, and that was even better!

Trainer Angelo Dundee told me:

Sure I deliberately made the split in the glove worse, but I was just doing my job as a professional and looking after my man. Henry was gracious enough to tell me some time later that given the same circumstances he would've expected his manager Jim Wicks to have done the same thing. Jim was big friends with my brother, Chris, and he asked him to pass me the message, 'Tell Angelo he's a rascal... but I would like him in my corner.' Boxing's a dog-eat-dog sport, and you have to be ready to use every trick in the book. It's not a sport for priests and rabbis. You have to park your conscience and do what has to be done to get across that victory line.

The torn glove became the most famous in boxing and, a few days later, I saw it on display at the Soho betting shop run by the notorious Albert 'Italian Al' Dimes, a long-time pal of The Bishop through their gambling obsession. Jim always stressed that their friendship had nothing to do with Albert's well-documented criminal activities, which included ruling the underworld turf later claimed by the Krays and a knife fight with his bitter rival Jack Spot in 1955 that has gone down in gangland legend. 'Albert's a pussycat,' said Jim, looking as if butter would not melt in his mouth. 'He only takes liberties against those who take liberties against him.'

Both gloves were later signed by Clay/Ali and Henry, and in 2001 advertising executive Trevor Beattie – who masterminded the FCUK campaign for French Connection – bought them at auction for £37,600. This was the little matter of £7,600 more than Henry earned for the fight. I can almost hear Henry saying: 'Fcuk me!'

WAR IN EUROPE

A lot of people thought Henry would retire after his almost glorious defeat by Clay. A lot of people were proved wrong. Those who thought he was set up for life had no idea of his tax liabilities and how the greengrocery business was draining his finances. He still had world title ambitions and there was the w-h-o-l-e of Europe to conquer.

By the time his eye healed after the bloody showdown with Clay, the European championship had become vacant following the retirement of Swede-basher Ingemar Johansson. Henry was matched with old foe Brian London for the European crown at Manchester Belle Vue on 24 February 1964 and he gave such a boxing exhibition that the fight could have been staged in the Tate Gallery. London was jabbed almost to a standstill on his way to a third defeat by the South London craftsman and the grounded Blackpool Bomber was sporting enough to say at the end of fifteen one-sided rounds: 'Henry, you've won me outright and can take me home and put me on your mantelpiece!'

Instead of bringing them satisfaction, the European title gave Henry and manager Jim Wicks nothing but aggravation.

I was so proud to win the European title to go with two Lonsdale Belts outright, but sadly it was to prove a pain in the arse. My third fight with London was very nearly called off at the last minute. We had a right old bust-up with the British Boxing Board of Control officials in the dressing-room when they tried to restrict the amount of bandage on my hands.

It was the angriest I ever saw Jim. He blew his top and told promoter Harry Levene that we were not going ahead with the fight. They had sprung on us at the last minute that there was a new rule on how much bandage was allowed, but they had made a cock-up with the calculation and were trying to limit me to half the permitted length. A boxer's hands are the tools of his trade and need protecting as much as possible. Levene, aware that he had a contract for the fight to go out live on BBC radio, measured the bandage himself and called the stewards every name under the sun because they'd got it wrong. The new length was much less bandage than we were used to and we banged up our left hand continually thumping it into London's face, and when the glove was pulled off after the fight, my hand quickly blew up to twice its normal size.

Having the European championship quickly gave us problems. The European Boxing Union treated boxers like puppets, dictating who you had to defend the title against and where and when. If you didn't jump – or fight – when they wanted you to, they'd have the title off you quicker than you could say Sugar Ray Robinson. In Jim Wicks they found a manager who would not just roll over and do what they demanded.

A problem at the time was that the main challengers for my title were all Germans and the top British promoters – Solomons and Levene – were not prepared to bring them over. In those days there were still some anti-German feelings about as a hangover from the war and the Jewish promoters were not going to be seen lining the pockets of German boxers and managers. So reluctantly we agreed to go back to Germany to defend the championship against southpaw Karl Mildenberger after the fight had been put out to purse offers by the EBU. Jim called them Effing Bleedingwell Useless.

When I started training for the contest, I felt a recurrence of the arthritic pain I often suffered in my left elbow. Two specialists told me I needed to rest it for at least two weeks. The German promoter, egged on by the EBU, was suspicious to the point of disbelieving. So we summoned him and an EBU representative to London and showed them X-rays and specialist reports. The promoter reacted by saying he would postpone the fight for two weeks, which was useless to us because it would have meant me going into the ring having lost two weeks' vital training.

Jim exploded and told the promoter what he could do with his new date, and the EBU reacted by stripping us of the title. They nominated Mildenberger to fight for the suddenly vacant championship against a mediocre Italian called Sante Amonti, who was knocked out in round one in Berlin. Not long afterwards Mildenberger was injured when due to defend his title and he was given a month's grace to get fit. So you can imagine why we were fighting mad with the inconsistent EBU!

Distracted by the verbal punch-up with the EBU, Henry was not in the right frame of mind for his next fight at the Royal Albert Hall on 16 November 1964 and he dropped a points decision to an ordinary American opponent, Richard Rischer, of whom *Who's Who* said

Who? He had been hand-picked to just give our hero a workout, but he came to wrestle rather than box and put Henry out of his stride with spoiling tactics that turned this into a mauling mess of a fight. Rischer's points victory was jeered by a disappointed crowd and Jim Wicks was honest enough to admit: 'We stank the place out.' Then the inevitable malapropism: 'We were very lackadaisy.' And lackadaisical, too.

Henry returned to the scene of the 'crime' two months later and there was an improved aroma when he produced the trusted left hook to stop Dick Wipperman – 'the wild buffalo from Buffalo' – in five rounds.

The next stop: Wolverhampton Civic Hall, where on 20 April 1965 he knocked American Chip Johnson cold in the first round. This whirlwind victory gave Henry particular satisfaction, because it avenged a third round defeat of his brother George, who was so badly cut by Johnson's fists that he decided to hang up his gloves and concentrate full-time on his trade as a master plasterer. He kept alive his interest in boxing by helping to train Henry and working in his corner.

Henry returned to the Midlands on 15 June 1965 for an open-air fight at Birmingham City's St Andrew's football stadium that captured the nation's interest. In the opposite corner was local hero Johnny Prescott, one of a queue of good-quality British heavyweights chasing Henry's title in the 1960s.

He was nicknamed the Beau Brummell of Birmingham because of his good looks, sharp dress sense and his liking for the ladies. Johnny was often photographed with the notorious Mandy Rice-Davies wrapped around him and I used to wonder how he ever got the energy for fighting. Well, I would think that, wouldn't I?

Mind you, I reckon Johnny deserved any luck and good times that came his way after the lousy hand fate had dealt him in his early days. When he was just two, his father died on the Dunkirk beaches while serving with the Tank Corps and his mother was killed in an air raid. Johnny was sent to an orphanage until he was thirteen, when an uncle took him into his home.

He started taking boxing seriously while doing his National Service in the army as a physical training instructor and he boxed for England as an amateur in 1961 before turning professional. In his first two years punching for pay, Prescott racked up a score of victories including eight clean knockouts. He had been beaten just once in twenty-three starts when in 1963 he came up against the first of his Coopers – George/Jim, who destroyed him in two rounds.

Three months later Prescott had an even bigger disaster when his former sparring partner Alex Barrow, a big-punching Nigerian, pulverised him in just 100 seconds.

Prescott got another hiding when he returned to the dressing-room, this time from his veteran manager George Biddles, who went at him hammer and tongue. He told him: 'You're paying the price for being too much of a good-time Charlie! If you want to get anywhere in this business you had better start becoming less of a ladykiller and more of a killer in the ring.'

The Biddles broadside had the desired effect and in his next fight Prescott avenged the defeat by Barrow. He followed this with two memorable battles against the highly touted new 'Golden Boy' of British boxing, the Blond Bomber from West Ham, Billy Walker. Prescott was stopped in the tenth and last round of their first thrilling fight and then got off the canvas to win the return on points.

Biddles then kept up a non-stop publicity campaign to get Henry to put up his titles against Prescott. 'Britain needs a new, young heavy-weight champion,' he said over and over again like a broken record.

'The boxing public is fed up with the Cooper-Erskine-London monopoly of the championship.'

I guess Biddles had a point. I had made five successful defences of the British and Commonwealth titles since taking them from Brian London in 1959. Three had been against Joe Erskine, another against London and I had knocked out Dick Richardson.

I was now an 'old man' of thirty-one and I was itching for a first notch on a third Lonsdale Belt when Biddles got his wish and steered Prescott into a challenge against me. He had managed to make 27-year-old Johnny sound like a fresh, young challenger. It was spin worthy of The Bishop.

Our fight at St Andrew's was delayed for two days because of torrential rain. I was more anxious than I would normally have been because I was carrying the secret that Jim had started negotiations for me to challenge Muhammad Ali/Clay for the world championship. I knew I dare not let Prescott win because it could wreck the plans and the chance I had dreamt of since I was a kid pretending to be Joe Louis.

Johnny had been specially coached for the fight by the great Jack Hood, a pre-war European welterweight champion whose ring skills had been legendary. Never saw Jack fight, but it was claimed he could go through an entire round without an opponent laying a glove on him because of his feints, clever footwork and speed of thought and movement. His speciality was catching punches on his gloves and then countering. Johnny had learned his lessons well: for the first third of the fight his defensive work was excellent and he stopped me landing any really telling blows.

But then, when I switched my point of attack from the head to the body, he started to visibly slow and I could hear him grunting as my punches sank deep into his midriff. 'Aye aye,' I thought, 'perhaps Johnny is still being a good-time Charlie.'

By the end of the tenth round he had taken three counts and was shifting a lot of punishment, and George Biddles wisely retired him despite Johnny's protests. I couldn't believe it when his fickle fans jeered and booed the decision to pull him out of what had become like a torture chamber for him and I gave them a rollocking on the MC's microphone. 'You should be cheering, not booing,' I told them. 'Johnny's a game boy and has taken a lot of punishment. He's done himself proud.'

As I finished speaking, the heavens opened up again and it started bucketing down with rain. If it had started half an hour earlier we would not have got the fight finished. Mind you, 'young' Johnny would have been in danger of drowning.

Much to the disgust and dismay of his former bookmaking associate Jack Solomons, Jim Wicks was working in harmony with Jarvis Astaire, Harry Levene and Mickey Duff to try and set up a world title fight with the former Cassius Clay, now demanding to be known as Muhammad Ali. Solomons got to hear about it on the boxing gossip-vine and called Wicks a traitor and a turncoat, or words to that effect. 'I'm doing what I think is best for Enery,' The Bishop said. 'If Jack wants to come up with something better, he knows my telephone number. In fact, he'll need to talk telephone numbers if he wants to improve on the deal we're getting.'

In a rage, Solomons instead started negotiating a world title challenge for Brian London. It was a hot-headed decision that would cost him a small fortune.

Henry carelessly dropped a ten rounds points decision to American journeyman Amos Johnson at Wembley Pool on 19 October 1965.

While a lacklustre performance, it strangely worked in Henry's favour. It convinced the Ali/Clay camp that he would be easy to take out in a world championship defence.

Henry was still the king of British boxing and he was honoured with a lunch at Buckingham Palace with HM The Queen and the entire Royal Family. An unashamed royalist, Henry described it as one of the proudest days of his life and he was able to give Prince Philip the exclusive news that a world title fight with Ali/Clay had been all but arranged for the spring of 1966.

'This Clay chappie,' Prince Philip asked, 'is it right his great-great-grandfather was a white Irishman?'

'So the story goes, sir,' said Henry. 'He has certainly got a lot of blarney about him.'

Rubbing shoulders with royalty and celebrities was the cream of Henry's life, but boxing remained his bread and butter and he was working harder than ever in the gymnasium in the knowledge that a world title shot was just around the corner. Jim Wicks always kept Henry up to speed with his negotiations and told him he had been assured by Ali's new masters – headed by National Islam leader Elijah Muhammad – that the title fight was on Ali's agenda.

Henry comfortably won back-to-back fights against Americans Hubert Hilton (a tenth-round stoppage) and Jefferson Davis (first round knockout) early in the New Year to clinch the fight night of his life.

Cassius Clay was coming back to town, only this time answering to the name of Muhammad Ali. And that was not blarney.

ROUND 8

ALI AND THE UNKINDEST CUT OF ALL

To convey the compelling story of the most important fight night in Henry's career, I retreat to a neutral corner and let Henry take over. This was how he described the build-up to the second Clay fight – or perhaps that should be the first fight with Muhammad Ali…

Cassius Clay or Muhammad Ali – to be honest, I didn't care what he called himself as long as he was there to answer the first bell and give me a shot at his world title. The fact that I was on a nice little earner was a bonus, but I would have fought for peanuts for a chance of getting my hands on the championship.

Clay's name – or rather, Ali's – had become like poison to many people in the United States. Since we had last fought he had publicly announced his allegiance to the Black Muslims and was refusing to be drafted into the US Army for war duty in Vietnam, citing his religious beliefs.

I admired his principles but struggled to understand his logic. By brilliant self-projection, showmanship and superb boxing skills he had made the name Cassius Clay known throughout the world. Now he disowned the identity because it had belonged to a white plantation boss who had enslaved his ancestors. I thought at the time that he had as much chance of becoming known and recognised as Muhammad Ali as I had of being called Shirley Temple.

But it shows how wrong you can be because within a year or so he was universally known as Muhammad Ali and now – all these years on – I come across youngsters who think that Cassius Clay and Muhammad Ali were two different people. Call me Shirley.

Mind you, in a way I guess they were two different people because although the Ali who filled Clay's boots had just as much to say for himself, a lot of the fun had gone out of him as he became poisoned by politics and bigoted thoughts. Instead of the old banter and blarney to try to get bums on seats, he was trying to convert people to his way of thinking with what amounted to sermons and hard-line political speeches. Thanks to the influence of Albina I had converted to Roman Catholicism, but I didn't go around shoving my beliefs down people's throats.

Many cynics were doubting his sincerity, but I'm sure it went much deeper than just trying to get out of fighting in Vietnam – his 'I've got no quarrel with them Vietcong' quote put a lot of white Americans in lynching mood and his stance was costing him an absolute fortune in lost commercial and endorsement contracts.

Leading up to our fight he had got himself heavily involved with Black Power spokesman Michael X and then Black Muslim leader Elijah Muhammad, whose son Herbert took over Ali's management after he had broken with the syndicate of white Kentucky businessmen who had handled him in his early years as a professional. Some saw it as out of the frying pan and into the fire.

In fact it was Michael X who made the first approach about staging a world title fight in Britain between Ali and me. Jim Wicks gave him short shrift and told him he would be dealing with Harry Levene, Mickey Duff and entrepreneur Jarvis Astaire, who held the ace card because of his Viewsport company that was a pioneer of closed-circuit promotions. This, of course, was way before satellite TV. Just imagine what we could have earned had there been pay-per-view television then!

The contest was beamed live to cinemas and theatres in every major city in Britain apart from London. Ali was on a guaranteed £100,000 purse – a huge amount at the time – plus considerable ancillary rights, such as North and South American closed-circuit income and television, radio and film rights. It was the most successful promotion in the history of British boxing.

I was on my best-ever payday of a guaranteed £50,000, plus a percentage of the European and Far East TV and closed-circuit takings. It may not sound a fortune in these days when world champions can demand millions of dollars but believe me, it was tasty take-home pay in that pre-decimalisation era.

We attracted 45,000 spectators to Highbury – home of my favourite football team, Arsenal – and hundreds of thousands watched the fight on screens in places like Tokyo, Bangkok, Dortmund, Buenos Aires, Mexico City and Manchester. I don't kid myself they were queuing up to see me, but the legend that was, uh, Muhammad Ali, even though most people continued to refer to him as Cassius Clay in the build-up for our fight. Many of them were willing me to land my left hook on his chin again, and I was told that the majority of viewers in America – the white ones – were supporting me. Fancy being hated in your own country. Thank goodness I've never experienced that and always fed off my wonderful home support.

Despite the spiteful Press treatment he had been getting in the United States, Ali received a rapturous welcome on his arrival in

London. There was no doubting his popularity was, if anything, on the increase outside his homeland, and he commented quietly and not in his publicity drum-beating way: 'I've been driven out of my own country because of my religious beliefs, yet every other country in the world welcomes me. It's a strange feeling. All I ask is the same treatment and respect in my country as other boxers and athletes get from Uncle Sam.'

When it was pointed out to him that other American boxers and athletes were not refusing to join the US Army, he replied: 'My religion is against war and I am within my legal and moral rights to claim exemption on the basis of being a Conscientious Objector. If I weren't the heavyweight champion of the world there would be none of this fuss. While I'm here in Britain I don't want to be bothered with questions about my personal affairs, such as the draft case and my divorce. I'm here to defend my title and that old man Henry Cooper had better watch out. I'm feeling real mean.'

In the countdown to the fight, that memorable moment when I floored the then Cassius Clay in the fourth round at Wembley was replayed on television and in cinemas scores of times. While it helped sell tickets, it worked against me in a way because every time it came on the screen or a photograph of the knockdown was reproduced in a newspaper it reminded Ali of the main danger to him. My left hook, my 'Ammer.

I knew this was going to make it that much harder to land my main weapon. There was no way Ali was going to forget to duck because he was getting constant reminders of what could happen if he exposed his chin for a split second, as he had at Wembley. In training I practised feinting with my left and landing with my weaker right hand, but I knew my best chance still lay with the good old left hook. To be honest, I couldn't hurt a fly with my right.

Ali had successfully twice defended his title following his farce of a return fight with Liston in Maine when Old Sonny went down and out to what most of us in the trade thought was a phantom punch. He had since stopped former champion Floyd Patterson in twelve rounds in Las Vegas and he convincingly outpointed rough, tough Canadian George Chuvalo over fifteen rounds in Toronto three months before our fight.

Both Ali and I showed we meant business by coming into the ring built for speed. Ali tipped the scales at 14st 3.5lb, which was the lightest he ever weighed as champion, shifting thirteen pounds from when he had beaten Chuvalo just two months earlier. He had really got himself into shape, which I suppose was a compliment to me. I weighed in at 13st 4lb and felt as slim and as fit as a thoroughbred greyhound, without a surplus ounce on me. I knew I was going to need to be at my most mobile for this fight-night of my life. No need this time for Jim Wicks to lead-weight me to a higher poundage.

Ali had refused to sign the contract for the voluntary defence of his championship until promoter Harry Levene guaranteed a largest-possible twenty-foot ring. Harry moaned like hell because he had to have one specially made at what was then a hefty cost of five hundred quid. It was a crafty move by Ali: he wanted as much room in which to manoeuvre as possible. Years earlier, Rocky Marciano had demanded a postage-stamp-size sixteen-foot ring when defending against one of my heroes, Don Cockell, from down the road from me at Battersea. The harder the punch you carry, the smaller the ring you require because it means you can get to your opponent quicker. In that phone-box of a ring, poor old Don had nowhere to hide. Ali had chosen a ring in which we could have had a five-a-side football match. The left hook I had landed back in 1963 obviously left a permanent mark on his memory, and he wanted as much room as possible in which to take evasive action.

I was chuffed to be in the Arsenal home dressing-room. You could almost feel the history of the place where old idols like Alex James, Ted Drake, the Compton brothers and more recently George Eastham and Joe Baker had changed. Now I was getting ready to follow in their footsteps, but to use my fists rather than my feet. I had got into the habit of openly praying and crossing myself before leaving the dressing-room and I had taped under the lace of my left boot small religious medallions that had been given to me by Albina and her Aunt Maria. In my short prayer I just asked God to keep me safe and help me do my best. I never asked for victory, just that I came through it all right. Winning was up to me.

I was almost carried into the ring on a wave of emotion from a huge crowd making as much noise as if good old Arsenal had scored a goal. I was nicely nervous and in perfect mood for the challenge. My preparations had been flawless and I honestly felt I could cause an upset against hot favourite Clay – sorry, Ali.

The last thing I did before the main floodlights were switched off was to wave to Albina who, for the one and only time in my career, was in a ringside seat watching me fight.

She hated every moment of it and hardly appreciated that this big fight atmosphere was the most electric and exciting that I'd ever experienced.

The action sat in Henry's memory bank like a Technicolor horror movie shot in crimson red. His brave challenge ended – perhaps predictably – in a sea of blood after one minute thirty-eight seconds of the sixth round. It was a nightmare repeat of their first meeting, but this time without the heart-stopping drama of a knockdown.

The simple, sad fact is that, as we all dreaded, the scar tissue around Henry's eyes was too susceptible and all too easy a target for Ali's slashing punches.

From the emotional singing of the national anthem, there had been an air of optimism over Highbury that matched any from the Herbert Chapman days in the 1930s when Arsenal dominated League football. Everybody was trying to transmit their energy and expectations to Henry as Jim Wicks, trainer Danny Holland and brother George climbed out of the ring, leaving our hero a lonely, proud figure up there in his corner awaiting the first bell.

Albina, looking like a trapped prisoner, immediately looked away as Ali and Henry advanced towards each other. Alongside her, legends of the ring Rocky Marciano and Georges Carpentier leaned forward, eager to see if the modern boxers could match their deeds. Further along the row, the three greatest Welsh actors of their generation – Stanley Baker, Donald Houston and Richard Burton, all friends of Henry – chorused their support.

For five rounds Henry forced the pace as Ali skipped and danced his way around the ballroom-size ring, the long laces on his snow-white boots twirling as he showed off the Ali Shuffle. Once, twice, maybe three times Henry got home with the left hook that had dumped the then Cassius Clay on the canvas in their first meeting. But instead of going down, Ali had the presence of mind to grab and hold while his head cleared before getting back on his bike and into his rhythmic retreat behind long, stabbing punches that were worryingly catching Henry in his tracks.

The bloody climax came with the dramatic suddenness of a landslide, just as we were thinking that Henry was on safe ground and everything was going reasonably well. As Henry tried to cut off Ali's retreat and drive him into a neutral corner, he was suddenly met with an avalanche of short left- and right-hand punches to the face. It was a blur of combination punches that come from only the greatest fighters, and as Ali turned Henry on to the ropes, ringsiders were sprayed with blood gushing from a wide-open gash along the so often vulnerable left eyebrow.

A sideways glance showed that Albina was hiding her face behind her fight programme, wanting to be anywhere but at that ringside watching her husband suddenly looking like the victim of a razor attack. Jim Wicks, Danny Holland, brother George and matchmaker Mickey Duff were like a poorly tuned barbershop quartet as they screamed from the corner for Henry to make one last desperate attempt to land the 'Ammer. But he was now blinded by a curtain of his own blood and missing wildly.

The roars from the crowd had gone from optimistic support to wild rage, because many thought that a butt caused the damage. Even Henry made that instant allegation, until he saw replays that showed the injury was definitely the result of a fusillade of deadly accurate punches.

There were soon cries of 'Stop it, ref!' mixed in with the angry growls as Henry's blood ran like a red river down his chest, darkening his royal-blue shorts. Ali showed no mercy, and even though he later said he hated doing it, he continued to pour punches into the widening wound. This was the bloodsport of boxing at its most terrifying and repellent.

It was an astonishing turn-around. Barely a minute earlier Henry had been more than holding his own and was ahead on many scorecards. Now here he was drenched in his own blood.

Scottish referee George Smith, his shirt turning crimson, ushered Ali to a neutral corner and needed just a perfunctory inspection of the damage to wave the fight over. Henry punched the air in disgust and frustration, and let fly with an expletive that edit-suite techni-cians carefully removed.

The dream was over, submerged beneath rivers of his blood, of becoming the first British-born fighter to win the world heavyweight title since New Zealand-based Bob Fitzsimmons back in 1897. Yes, this was the unkindest cut of all.

In that sixth round we had been boxing at long-range for about half a minute when he caught me as we both moved forward to launch punches, and as he moved away to continue his dance routine I felt blood oozing from a cut over my left eye. Immediately after the fight I told reporters there had been a clash of heads.

I was not accusing the champion of doing it deliberately; he never was that type of dirty fighter. But my honest opinion was that the damage had been caused by his head. There was so much blood flow-ing that I could not believe it had been done by punches. Ali threw a right hand as I was coming in and something hard hit me – in the heat of the battle I thought he'd butted me. Afterwards, looking at the film, I could see I had made a mistake and I later apologised to Ali for coming to the wrong conclusion.

It was in the moment just after the right hand landed that our heads came together, leading me into thinking the injury had been caused by a butt. In the heat of battle you don't always get the sequence of things right, and on this occasion I admit I was wrong.

He threw a left and a right, shortening his punches, and the effect as I came forward was a chopping blow on my eye with the heel of his glove. The eyebrow immediately split wide open.

It was the worst cut I ever had in boxing, deeper and longer even than in my first fight with him. Nobody had to tell me it was a bad cut. I knew at once that I was in desperate trouble. I could feel the warm blood gushing down my face and on to my shoulders and chest; it was really blinding me, and was like trying to see through a red-stained window. I was not aware of any pain, just frustration that my old jinx had struck again and in the most important fight of my life. And I was also angry because I thought, wrongly, that Ali had opened the cut with his head.

Ali said afterwards that because of his religious beliefs he did not want to cause me any more damage and so laid off, but if you ever see the film you'll notice he pounced like a panther, landing as many punches on the eye as he could. I'm not knocking him for it because that's the fight game for you, but I just wish he had not come across as hypocritical. I really liked the bloke, and that nonsense did him no favours with the many people who wanted to see me shut his big mouth.

As in our first fight, I was left thinking about what might have been. Most judges at the end either had me dead level or just in front on points, and I knew I had plenty in reserve. It was the fittest I'd ever been in my life. In eleven rounds of boxing Ali had never had me in serious trouble apart from the cuts. I'd had him down once and had won more rounds than I'd lost.

I often wonder what I could have achieved but for the cut-eye curse. But it's no use crying over spilt blood.

Jim Wicks got taken in by Henry's instant assertion that a butt had caused the damage and said in the dressing-room afterwards: 'Clay or whatever he calls himself nutted us. If he's the religious gentleman he likes us to think, he'll give us a return. In our two fights, he's hardly won a round.'

Across the marble halls of Highbury, in the visitors' dressing-room Ali was holding court. 'Henry hurt me just once,' he told reporters. 'He caught me a good left hook in the third round, but I was far too fast for him tonight and he could not follow up. I opened the cut with a left-right combination. Henry is a man of honour and I'm sure that once he gets over the disappointment of his defeat he'll accept that I did not cause the damage with my head. With as pretty a face as I have, do you think I'd go around butting opponents? Man, my one idea is to keep my good looks and want nobody's head anywhere near my face. As soon as I opened the cut I wanted the referee to stop it; the blood disturbed me a lot. It was pure violence, and that's against my personal feelings and my religion. Henry's a good fighter but his flesh is weak. Tell the old boy it's time to call it a day. He has fought with honour, but he's a bleeder and always will be.'

Ali returned to London later in the summer of 1966 and polished off Brian London in three rounds on a Jack Solomons promotion at Earls Court that was a financial flop. The Blackpool boxer could never capture the public support like Our Enery. He lacked that special Cooper charisma.

Henry had expert and expensive plastic surgery on his damaged eye while he considered his future. Albina, shaken by her first and only experience of seeing him fight (well, she looked for at least a minute from behind her programme), wanted him to hang up his gloves, but did not try to interfere in a decision she knew he had to make for himself. He talked it through with The Bishop and decided there was still plenty to fight for: he wanted a third Lonsdale Belt outright and he felt the need to win back the European crown that had been taken away from him without a fight.

Our Enery – with everybody anticipating his farewell to the fight game – fought on for another four and a half years!

ROUND 9

FREUDIAN FLOYD AND THE BLOND BOMBER

Floyd Patterson was a charming but complicated man, whose psychological problems earned him the nickname Freudian Floyd. The depths of his haunting self-doubt are best illustrated by the fact that he disguised himself with a beard and dark glasses because he was so ashamed of the first of his two one-round defeats by Sonny Liston, who violently wrenched the world heavyweight title from him.

When he was at ease with himself and boosted by self-belief there were few better-equipped fighters in ring history. Just Henry's luck that he was brimming with confidence and assurance when they met at Wembley Arena on 20 September 1966.

Jim Wicks admitted worrying through sleepless nights before agreeing that Patterson was the right opponent for Henry's come-back after his bloody world championship challenge against Ali. 'We wanted to keep in the world title picture,' The Bishop said. 'Patterson had been a good champion, but we thought he was past his best after his defeats by the animal Liston and then he got a hammering from Ali. But we got it wrong.' Henry was knocked out by what he later described as the greatest punch he never saw, a right to the jaw that travelled with the speed of light and literally knocked our hero sideways.

From the day I watched Patterson win the Olympic middleweight gold medal at the 1952 Olympics, I knew he had fast fists. In fact they were among the fastest in history. If he'd had a stronger chin and more belief in himself, he would have gone down in history as one of the all-time great heavyweight champions.

My plan was to test his jaw with the good old left hook, but he was too shrewd to give me an opening, keeping his right glove covering his chin and countering from behind his famous peek-a-boo guard. Near the end of the third he let loose with a combination, finishing with a left hook, and I was forced to take a brief count.

He had me over again in the fourth round with a flurry of punches that were just a blur. I got myself up inside the ten seconds but was not really in full control of my senses. Next thing I knew I had a crowd of anxious faces peering down at me and Jim was asking, 'You all right, son?'

I'd been knocked sparko by a cracking right out of the blue that landed so hard I turned over on my way to the canvas. I can only tell you all this because I later saw it on film. At the time I honestly did not know what had hit me. Didn't see it, didn't feel it.

Patterson was a wonderful sportsman and was genuinely concerned for me, and I appreciated that. We are all warriors when the bell goes, but there's no need for nastiness and boasting once a fight is over. You'll be surprised at the camaraderie of old opponents. There is nothing like boxing for earning respect. Like me, Floyd had converted to Roman Catholicism and was a good and caring man. I might have fought him for the world title back in 1959 but politics got in the way and Brian London got the shot. Floyd knocked him out in eleven one-sided rounds, so he did a pretty good job on us Brits!

It is pointless trying to make excuses because Floyd had beaten me good and proper, but we were concerned about the pain I was continually getting from my left elbow and I had lots of hush-hush specialist treatment to try to sort it out.

Albina and I never talked boxing at home. Once the door was shut we got on with our family life, but for the first time she let on that she was worried sick about me and wanted me to pack it in. Jim got to hear about it and told her a bit too bluntly for Albina's taste that she should keep out of it. That was a bit of a touchy time.

Anyway, I gave it a few weeks and then after a long chat with Jim I decided to carry on because I still had my eye on a record third Lonsdale Belt and also the European title. And, let's be honest, there was still good money to be earned. Albina was not best pleased, but she went along with it because it was what I wanted.

Henry made his return to the ring at Leicester on 17 April 1967, and he gave one of his most lethargic performances on the way to an uninspiring ten rounds points victory over unranked American Boston Jacobs. This was planned as a warm-up for his next target: completing the two title defences he needed to win a history-setting third Lonsdale Belt. First up, Jack Bodell.

Billed as 'the chicken farmer from Swadlincote', Bodell was one of the most awkward heavyweights ever to step into a British ring. A lumbering, thickset, craggy-jawed southpaw, he relied on bullying brawn over brain to get the better of intimidated opponents.

He had biffed and bashed his way into the No. 1 contender's role and so Jim Wicks had to reluctantly agree to the defence, providing one of his classic lines in the build-up to the fight: 'Bodell and all them other southpaws should have been drowned at birth. They are a detergent to the fight game.'

The contest was staged at Molineux, famous home of the Wolverhampton Wanderers Football Club, on 13 June 1967, and the crowd of 10,000 got excited when their Midlands hero swarmed all over Henry in a wild first round. What his supporters failed to realise is that Henry had deliberately held back in the opening three minutes, letting his cumbersome opponent use up energy as he saved his big guns for the right moment.

Bodell came charging out for the second round in his bull-in-a-china-shop style and this time, instead of retreating and defending, Henry stood his ground and caught him with a full-blooded left hook that knocked the suddenly stupefied Derbyshire giant back on to the ropes. The referee came to Bodell's rescue as a follow-up attack knocked him through the ropes, his senses completely scattered. Henry's hook had lost none of its raw power and potency. It had once been measured by scientists to travel at thirty miles per hour over a distance of six inches, landing with the acceleration equal to sixty times the force of gravity. At the climax of the fight, Jack Bodell was in no shape to do the maths.

Henry and Albina's second son, John Pietro, arrived on 5 August 1967 to complete the happy Cooper family, and no sooner had Henry Marco got used to having a little brother than their dad was off again training for his next fight. Waiting in the opposite corner at Wembley Arena on 7 November 1967 was the Blond Bomber from West Ham, Billy Walker.

Billy was, to use an East Endism, 'as game as a bagel'. Those many mimics who did me the honour of impersonating me always used my old line, 'He's a good strong boy.' That really summed up Billy, who never minded taking two, three or four punches to get one in of his own. He fought a bit too much with his face for my taste, but there is no denying that his biff-bang-wallop style won him many fans.

They dubbed him the 'Golden Boy' of British boxing and there was nobody to touch him as a ticket-seller. His name on the bill almost guaranteed a sell-out at any London venue. He was brilliantly guided by his brother George, a former light-heavyweight title challenger who invested all the money they earned with such vision that he became a high-powered City tycoon with his fingers in worldwide business ventures.

Along with everybody else, I liked Billy. He was a smashing bloke with tons of charisma. Advertisers also liked him and he had a glamorous image that brought him endorsement contracts for things like clothes and hairdressing cream. I asked Jim if he could get me a sponsor for the polishing of bald heads. Jim had a lovely bald dome, while my hair was receding so quickly I couldn't even do a Bobby Charlton comb-over.

Though I couldn't compete with Billy in the barnet department, I frankly didn't think he was in my league as a fighter and I was convinced I would have the beating of him in a fight that was billed as: 'Who's the King of the Cockneys?'

Billy and I got on fine in the build-up to the fight, managing to stay reasonably pleasant for two blokes about to try to knock each other's block off. But The Bishop and George Walker disliked each other on sight. They kept sniping at each other, George seeming to think he could wind me up by getting at old Jim, who was by then well into his seventies. Jim had seen it all and done it all, and gave better than he received in the verbal exchanges, and they were still going at it just before the bell rang to start the real fight.

My plan was to soften Billy up with left jabs for the first half of the fifteen-rounder and then open up with my heaviest artillery from about the seventh round. I had used similar tactics against Johnny Prescott with good effect. Walker and Prescott had knocked hell out of each other in two back-to-back battles in 1963 and I don't think either of them was ever quite the same force after they had severely punished each other. Johnny was the better boxer, but Billy was the more dangerous puncher and could really take a whack on the jaw.

I knew it was pointless trying to knock Billy out early doors. I just might have banged up my hands trying to finish him, so I concentrated on boxing him and making sure I didn't get caught by one of his famous haymakers. The trouble for Billy was you could see his big right-hand punch coming a mile away. He used to telegraph it and it was easy to step inside or block it, and to counter with a left to his unguarded head. He might just as well have announced over the ring microphone, 'I'm about to throw my right hand.'

Everything went perfectly to plan. I kept pumping out the old trombone left and Billy kept eating it up. His defence was all over the place and every time he set himself for one of his roundhouse rights, I just knocked him off balance with a left lead.

A lot of the newspaper experts had predicted that Billy would cut me up with his rough, tough tactics, but ironically it was the East Ender whose flesh was weak. I opened an inch-long slit over his eye and in the eighth round I landed a stream of left jabs on the injury. I was making the eye the target. I know that sounds terrible, but boxing's not a game, it's a business – a bloody hard business often with the law of the jungle. I was doing exactly what Ali had done to me in our two fights and the referee stopped it in the eighth, with Billy in a right old state.

It was a victory that gave me huge satisfaction because I was now the proud owner of a record three Lonsdale Belts.

Henry now reigned supreme over British heavyweights and had seen off the cream of the crop (Hungarian-born Joe Bugner had just left school). Jim Wicks said: 'There's nobody left in Britain for us to beat. Time for us to go back into Europe, Enery.'

Another European adventure was about to start. 'Yeah,' agreed Henry. 'Let's go for it.' All right, it wasn't exactly Napoleonesque, but Our Enery was much more of a Wellington.

And a certain German champion was about to meet his Waterloo.

ROUND 10

EUROPEAN EMPEROR

Belted in the nicest possible way, the Cooper-Wicks team switched their sights from the domestic scene to a European path they had trodden before with a mixture of triumph and frustration. It still got under their skin that the EBU had taken the European title away from them without a punch being thrown and had virtually handed it to the Dortmund southpaw, Karl Mildenberger.

Come September 1968, Mildenberger was still the title-holder and once Henry had recovered from a knee cartilage operation, promoter Harry Levene buried his anti-German feelings to coax the champion to come to Wembley Arena for a long-awaited showdown with the British and Commonwealth king.

I asked Levene how he had reconciled paying a purse to a German boxer, having refused to even consider it in the past. 'Believe me, I don't like paying this Kraut,' he told me, 'but I know I am going to have the satisfaction of seeing Henry give him a bloody good hiding.'

Levene got a shoal of hate mail from the Jewish fraternity, who considered it disgraceful that he was lining the pocket of

Mildenberger and many regular Jewish ringsiders boycotted the fight. Henry always remained above politics and just got on with his job.

Mildenberger was a hefty and powerful all-rounder who could box cagily from long range and also thump hard with follow-through lefts after finding the range with his southpaw right lead. He had proved a handful for Muhammad Ali before being stopped in the twelfth round of a world title bid in Germany in September 1966, following Ali's successful title defences against Cooper and London during a mop-up of European challengers.

A victory over Henry would have given Mildenberger a record seven consecutive successful defences of the European title, but he came up against a Cooper in dominating form and not at all ring-rusty after his long lay-off because of a dodgy knee.

Henry gave him quite a pasting – or perhaps a plastering – for eight rounds, dictating the pace and pattern of the fight with a left jab that was rarely out of the German's reddening and rapidly swelling face. Most boxers would look to use the right hand as the main weapon against a southpaw, but by clever use of the ring Henry was able to stop the German's advance with his awesome left.

Mildenberger got as frustrated as a bluebottle hitting a window as he continually failed to land any of his big bombs and he started to get reckless with his head. Henry came out of an eighth-round clinch with a gash over his eye and the Italian referee Nello Barroveccio – to the surprise of many – instantly disqualified the protesting German for butting.

I met up with Karl while working as a PR on the Ali-Dunn fight in Munich in 1976 and he told me: 'Henry was the best European opponent I met and he deserved his victory over me, but not in the way it finished. I did not deliberately catch him with my head, as was suggested: the cut was caused by my left hand, but it was on the blind side of the referee and I will never know how he managed to see it as a butt. I don't think he would have disqualified me anywhere else but in England. But I had no complaint against Henry. He was a true English gentleman and a good advertisement for boxing in the way he conducted himself, in and out of the ring.'

It was to prove Mildenberger's final fight and he hung up his gloves with the satisfaction of knowing he had been Germany's most successful heavyweight since the halcyon days of the legendary Max Schmeling.

Henry's year had got off to a proud start when he was awarded an OBE in the New Year's honours list. He drove himself to the Palace for the investiture in his favourite car, a Bentley Continental. This was his one selfish possession and a sign of how far he had come since his first car, the second-hand Ford Prefect he and George had bought for £100 in 1954 and in which they had had the frightening collision after the Joe Erskine fight of 1955. Henry admitted to being a car crank, getting a better and more powerful vehicle virtually after every major fight victory. He looked on it as a sort of reward, and his accountant cleverly (and legally) made it a business expense. His parade of cars over the years included top-of-the-range Ferraris and a Jensen Interceptor. Henry loved driving, and often motored to Italy through the Alps in France and Switzerland with Albina and the boys. He was close friends with former world F1 champion Graham Hill and was trained by him to take part in celebrity races, driving the Brands Hatch circuit at terrifying speeds. Henry said he got an even bigger adrenaline rush from the high-speed driving than from fighting.

He needed a safety belt when he made the next defence of his European title against notorious Italian wild man of the ring Piero Tomasoni, who was fittingly nicknamed 'The Axeman' because he used to swing his punches as if trying to chop down a tree. It was staged at Rome's Palazzo dello Sport on 13 March 1969 and developed into the most turbulent fight of Henry's career.

I had a worrying time throughout much of the late 1960s with a knee that gave me some terrible pain and prevented me from getting in my usual quota of road running. A cartilage operation seemed to have sorted it out and I went to Rome confident I could see off Tomasoni, a roughhouse fighter who didn't believe in taking prisoners. What I didn't realise is that he was not only a hard nut but also something of a nutcase!

Tomasoni had knocked out Jack Bodell at the Albert Hall earlier in the year, so we knew he could bang a bit. They'd had a real rough and tumble, and according to reports the Italian had been even more awkward than Bodell, who was hardly a ballet dancer of a fighter. So I should have known what to expect, but nobody could have planned for what happened in the ring that night.

The Palazzo dello Sport is an incredible arena. The stands climb up fifty feet in the air and making my entrance with the capacity crowd jeering and whistling made me feel as if I was entering a cockpit. I must have looked like a midget to the spectators up in the gods and the atmosphere was the sort they must have had in the old Colosseum.

Our tactics were to let Tomasoni burn himself out before we opened up. That meant tucking my chin in and keeping my left in his face, unbalancing him. He was a real shortarse, four inches shorter than me, and so I had to punch down all the time, which reduced my power.

All my fight plans went out of the window after I'd floored him in the first round with my first real hard left hook, delivered off a jab. From then on it was bedlam. When he got up he just went berserk and charged at me with his head down, using it like a third glove, throwing punches from all angles and without caring where they landed. Some were as low as my thigh, others landed on the back of my neck and in the kidneys. I looked to the Dutch referee Ben Bril, but he was in no mood to upset the screaming Roman fans. We felt as if we'd been thrown to the lions.

Tomasoni came roaring out of his corner at the start of the second round like a maniac and one right hand landed so low that it dented my aluminium cup guarding the family jewels. If I'd not been wearing the protection, I reckon I'd now be Miss Henrietta Cooper! I went down on my knees with my eyes watering and my unmentionables aching. I couldn't believe it when the referee started counting over me. Jim Wicks was up on the apron demanding that Tomasoni should be disqualified, but quickly got down when the fans started pelting him with rubbish.

I dragged myself up and started to unload my heaviest punches on a squat opponent who seemed as wide as he was tall. He was rushing at me like a wild bull. In the fourth round I caught him with a left hook and, as he fell down, he grabbed me and took me with him. Jack Solomons was sitting at the ringside and was brave enough to stand up and shout to the referee to at least warn Tomasoni, who was completely out of control.

As I regained my feet, he pulled himself up by hanging on to my waist, then immediately threw another low blow, which at last brought a warning from the referee. This was the signal for the fanatical Roman crowd to launch fruit, rotten tomatoes and lumps of salami into the ring, a lot of it coming from the top tiers way up in the sky. They must have thought I was a hungry fighter. Italians! Don't you just love 'em?

Blimey, I thought to myself, I'd better get this over quick because it will be their seats being thrown next. I finally managed to end Tomasoni's all-or-nothing challenge in the fifth round with a full-power left hook that lifted him off his feet before he slumped to the canvas, his eyes rolling. Somehow he got up as the count reached nine, but he was in no position to defend himself and the referee signalled a knockout before steering him on unsteady legs back to his corner, not knowing who or where he was. Jim Wicks leapt into the ring and said: 'Let's scarper as quick as possible. I think they want to lynch us.'

But funnily enough, once the fight was over the crowd suddenly swung their support to me and gave me a great ovation, perhaps remembering that I had an Italian wife. A pressman got hold of Albina soon after and told her how I had been hit low and roughed up before knocking out Tomasoni. She said she was so relieved and happy that I had made him pay for the foul punches and that he had brought shame on Italy.

Her quotes were twisted in the Italian papers to read that she was ashamed to be Italian and her family were given a rough time for a while. Jim told Albina that in future she should not say a word to the press, but to pass the calls on to him. It was a tough way to learn that you had to know which journalists you could trust. I got on with most of them, but there were some that Jim would not allow anywhere near me.

All the British ringside reporters in Rome were in agreement that they had not seen a rougher championship contest. How the referee didn't see Tomasoni's low blows I'll never know. Jim said he must have been watching a different fight. I showed my protector to the reporters after the fight and they were amazed to see it was concaved.

Peter Wilson, the legendary columnist with the *Daily Mirror*, described it as looking like an old sardine can that had been kicked in; he added in his report that he had never seen a fighter 'so wickedly fouled'. And Peter had witnessed hundreds of fights. But it was the first one where he had been whacked on the side of the face with an orange the size of a grapefruit while typing his report. He had a bigger bruise on his face than I did!

Donald Saunders of the *Daily Telegraph* told me he thought Rocky Marciano was the roughest fighter he had ever seen until he clapped eyes on Tomasoni. I was glad to get back to London in one piece – I had a date to keep at the Palace.

Our hero, with Albina proud as punch by his side, arrived at Buckingham Palace in his Bentley to receive his OBE and the Queen showed she was well informed by asking him about his knee. 'It's fine now, ma'am, after the operation,' he responded, little realising that he would soon be back under the surgeon's knife… and minus all three of his titles.

BUST-UP WITH THE BOARD OF CONTROL

Henry Cooper OBE carried a secret into the ring with him when he battled with the brawling Piero Tomasoni: he was being lined up for another world heavyweight title fight. Muhammad Ali had been stripped of the championship because of his refusal to join the US Army, citing his Islamic beliefs and claiming to be a Conscientious Objector.

Jimmy Ellis, Ali's chief sparring partner, won the WBA version of the championship at what was the start of the alphabet-soup diluting of the world titles. Negotiations were under way for him to defend his crown against Henry in London on a Jack Solomons promotion, when the British Boxing Board of Control announced they would veto the contest because they did not recognise the WBA.

Jim Wicks exploded with rage. 'What way is this to treat Britain's greatest boxing hero?' he complained to anybody who would listen. 'The Board is supposed to represent us, not be our enemy.'

Avoiding malapropisms and picking his words carefully, The Bishop announced: 'We're giving up our British and Empire titles in protest. The Board know where they can stick them. Our Enery has been their best earner for years. Now let's see how they get on without having their hands in our pockets.' I had never seen Jim so angry. He was almost purple with indignation, which come to think of it was a perfect hue for The Bishop.

Of course, Jim knew he and Henry had the European title to fall back on and could look to the Continent for lucrative defences as Henry moved into the autumn of his career. But first he was determined that they would go through with the world title fight with Ellis in an unsanctioned contest in either Rome or Dublin. If he could beat Ellis, it would open up the world market again.

But the best-laid plans of mice, men and boxers oft go astray. Henry's knee problem came back to haunt and hurt him, and as he was carted off to hospital for a cartilage operation he had to reluctantly surrender his European crown.

From being British, Empire (as it was then) and European heavyweight champion, our hero was suddenly bereft of any titles.

We couldn't believe it when the Board refused to get behind our world title bid. They tied us up with political tape, saying they didn't support the WBA version of the title but the New York one. I was really worried about Jim – he was so angry I thought he was going to have a stroke. Don't forget he was no longer a spring chicken, but a tough old geezer into his seventies.

I was choked that they were blocking my chance to challenge for the title. The one time in my career I needed them and they suddenly became invisible men. I knew in my heart that it was only the equivalent of half a world title, but half a loaf is better than none and I would have earned a nice crust against an opponent I was confident I could have beaten. Ellis was a useful boxer but not in the same class as Ali and Patterson. All these years later, people will wonder what the fuss is about, but back then we were still accustomed to just eight champions, one for each weight division. The alphabet boys hadn't taken over.

I had held the British and Empire titles since 1959 and had won a record three Lonsdale Belts outright. We thought the Board had treated us disgracefully after all the money they'd earned from our purses. We gave up the hard-earned titles to emphasise our disgust and then started training for a fight with Ellis that would have needed to be staged outside the Board's jurisdiction. Jack Solomons was talking about Dublin or Rome.

Then the old knee let me down again and I was in bloody agony. It was back to hospital and goodbye to my world title chance and also to my European championship. It all looked very depressing.

It was widely predicted that Henry would never fight again, but he battled back to fitness with daily treatment and training at his favourite Highbury football ground, getting himself into such good shape that Jim Wicks (very reluctantly) patched up his quarrel with the British Boxing Board of Control. They accepted his argument that Henry was the logical number one contender for his old British and Empire titles that had now passed into the southpaw hands of a former victim, Jack Bodell.

But before his return battle, Henry had to endure another rather more pleasing ordeal after being trapped by Eamonn Andrews and his Big Red Book. As a *This Is Your Life* scriptwriter for fourteen years, I knew the lengths they had gone to in their bid to keep the secret from him. Henry later told me it was one of the best, yet most nerve-wracking experiences of his life. 'Jim Wicks set me up good and proper and as Eamonn came into view, I said, "You old rascal," or words to that effect. You sit there dazed and bemused, wondering who the heck is going to come onto the set next. But it was a wonderful night and I just could not believe that Albina, Jim and George had kept the secret from me. What made it for me was when the boys, Henry Marco and John Pietro, came on. That really choked me up.'

Muhammad Ali sent a filmed message from the United States and among the studio guests were Henry's old opponents Billy Walker, Dick Richardson and the man who was going to be in the opposite corner for his next fight, Jack Bodell.

The chicken farmer from Swadlincote showed the heart of a lion when defending his titles at Wembley Arena on 24 March 1970. He sensibly kept his chin tucked into his chest to avoid a repeat of his two-round demolition in their previous meeting, but he was just not in the same class as Our Enery, who left handed his way to a well-deserved but hard-earned fifteen rounds points victory to get the first notch on a fourth Lonsdale Belt. In the dressing-room after the fight Henry had to have treatment to bruises on his shins and feet, where the cumbersome Bodell had continually trodden on him and kicked him in his clumsy attempts to overpower the older opponent.

A familiar face was missing in the dressing-room: trainer Danny Holland, who had worked with Henry throughout his professional career. He was recognised as the finest cuts man in the business, but he did not feel he was sufficiently rewarded for his skills and quit the camp after a bitter row with Jim Wicks over his wages. Former European welterweight champion Eddie Thomas, an experienced manager and cornerman, took Danny's place in the Cooper team.

'We had some good times with Danny,' Henry said. 'But these things happen in life. Don't forget professional boxing is a business. Jim and Danny had been at loggerheads for a long time and it was causing an atmosphere. I had virtually been training myself anyway, with the help of George, who continued to come to the gym with me and on training runs. It was sad to see Danny go, but it was not the big thing the press tried to make it.'

Many experts considered Henry was taking on more than he could handle when he climbed back into the Wembley Arena ring on 10 November 1970 to challenge the fearsome Jose Urtain for the European title he'd picked up after Cooper had been forced to relinquish it.

Urtain had won thirty-three of his thirty-five fights inside the distance and his only defeat was on a disqualification; thirty of his opponents had not got past the third round. On paper, it was a sensational record.

In all my time watching and following boxing I had never known anybody quite like Urtain. He came from the Basque country, around San Sebastián, and was a champion rock lifter, with a muscular physique that could have been hewn out of the Pyrenees. Jose followed a long line of Urtains, who were folk heroes in the Basque territory of North-East Spain. His grandfather once won an unofficial world's strongest man competition and Jose was considered equally strong, judged on the weight of rock he could lift with his bare hands. He also knew how to lift money from promoters and flatly refused to come to England to defend his title until Harry Levene agreed to pay what was then a record £50,000 purse. 'I've been mugged,' Harry moaned, after chasing the champion all over Spain to get his signature on a contract. 'I feel as if he's dropped one of his rocks on my head!'

At twenty-seven, Urtain was nine years Henry's junior and not too many punters fancied the veteran Londoner to win as he climbed into the ring to try and capture the European crown for a third time.

People feared for me because of Urtain's famous strength. But being a strong man doesn't necessarily mean you can fight. If that was the case, the bodybuilders and weightlifters would all be champions, but most of them are too muscle-bound to be able to throw punches.

Judging by Jose's record of knockouts he had a wicked punch, but when I looked through his list of opponents I had hardly heard of any of them. I felt sure he had got to the top on the back of a bum-of-the-month campaign. I was quietly confident I could make it curtains for Urtain.

I spent the first round feeling him out. He was stocky and built like a Spanish bull, with bulging biceps and powerful forearms that showed the evidence of his rock-lifting sideline. He was quickly swinging that right club of a fist of his but in such crude fashion that I was soon thinking to myself, 'Take your time, Henry. You've got a right mug here. Just don't do anything silly.'

As he huffed and puffed, I set about giving him a boxing lesson. It was real bull and matador stuff. I was stabbing long left leads into his face and moving inside his swings that were even more obvious than those that Billy Walker had been throwing at me. A lot of boxing is in the eyes and I could quickly see that Señor Urtain was suddenly not fancying the job. From giving me the hard-man stare when we touched gloves at the start, he was now looking down at his feet and taking hopeful lunges.

The only problem he gave me was with the dangerous use of his head and he opened a cut with an early charge; but Eddie Thomas was able to keep on top of it during the intervals, so it never really bothered me.

Urtain was tiring himself out throwing big right handers that were putting ringside spectators in more danger than me. It is more tiring to throw and miss than land punches. And he was doing a lot of missing. As he began to slow, I stepped up my pace and started to double up with the left jab, and then began to add the occasional hook that came in at an angle and bounced off his tough nut. He had little finesse but was as hard as iron. It was like punching a coconut.

There was just one scary moment in the fifth when he landed with a looping right to the body. It took my breath away, but I did not let on that I was hurt and let go with a two-fisted volley that stopped him in his tracks. From then on he dared not open up because he knew the moment he started to launch his right he was going to take two or three thumping lefts in the face.

I gave him a real shellacking in the eighth round and he was now peering at me through badly swollen eyes. It had got to the stage where I was almost hitting him at will and very little was coming back at me. Jose was clearly very relieved when the referee rescued him as I drove him back across the ring with a combination of hooks and crosses. He looked as if a ton of rocks had fallen on him.

Urtain was a classic example of a manufactured champion who had been fed a procession of pushovers and had not been able to learn his trade properly. He had all the equipment to become a top-quality champion, but had not been taught the fundamentals of the sport. It was one of my most satisfying victories.

Little did we know that it would also be the *last* of Henry's victories. Secretly, he and Jim decided on just one more fight. Waiting for him in the opposite corner was a young man from Bedford via Hungary, Joe Bugner.

It was going to be one of the most controversial contests in the history of British boxing.

ROUND 12

WELL AND TRULY BUGNERED

Win, lose or draw, Jim and Henry had quietly made up their minds that Joe Bugner would be the last opponent. Henry had fought the good fight and was now sensibly accepting that time had caught up with him; his body was sending out signals that it was finding the demands of training and fighting too much of a strain. The pain in his left elbow had become so bad that there were days when he could not even comb his hair, button his shirt or do up his shoelaces. He was having regular Harley Street treatment to get himself fit enough for one final fight, and against an opponent who had been a young boy in revolution-torn Hungary when Henry was already into the early stages of his professional ring career.

Not counting the brief period when he gave up the titles in protest over the Board of Control's lack of support, Henry had been champion of Britain and the Commonwealth for a remarkable span of twelve years and he was justifiably proud of the fact that he had taken on and beaten all-comers. Joe Erskine, Brian London, Dick Richardson, Johnny Prescott, Jack Bodell and Billy Walker, from a golden era of heavyweights, had each been given their chance to take the crowns and Henry had beaten them all. He had never ducked a challenger and he was determined that he was not going to let a relative novice like Bugner ruin his record.

Joe was just three days past his twenty-first birthday, while Henry was a couple of months short of his thirty-seventh. He had forgotten more than Bugner had learned about the hardest game (or, if you prefer, the sweet science) and was confident he could mess him about and cancel out the age difference by intelligent pacing and careful conservation of energy.

Despite being knocked out early in his career, Bugner had since proved he had a strong chin and Henry trained with a fifteen-round distance contest in mind. Standing 6ft 4in and weighing near to sixteen stone, Joe had a superbly sculptured physique. In his schooldays he was one of Britain's finest young discus throwers and he was built just like one of those statues of a Greek discus-throwing god. But there were many critics who thought he often used to seem as mobile as a statute in the ring and he was not a natural, instinctive fighter.

His manager, an intelligent, livewire Anglo-Scot called Andy Smith, had done a marvellous job in moulding and manufacturing him into an orthodox but predictable stand-up boxer. Andy had spotted Joe while he was still a schoolboy and, impressed by his physique and power, set about trying to shape him into a world-beater. Many saw Smith as something of a puppeteer and he was aided and abetted with the string-pulling by the shrewd matchmaking of Mickey Duff.

Bugner's life story was like something out of a Hollywood script-writer's imagination. He was born in Szeged in southern Hungary, not knowing his father, and was just six at the time of the 1956 Hungarian revolution that triggered an invasion by Russian troops. Joe's mother, with her son in tow, bravely joined the flood of refugees escaping from Hungary and they boarded a ship they thought was taking them to the United States. But they wound up in Britain, first of all in a refugee camp and then a family home in Bedfordshire, where Joe revealed his all-round sporting prowess. He was an outstanding schoolboy athlete, but it was not until he was fifteen that he showed any interest in boxing. Just two years later he was making his professional debut under Andy Smith's guidance.

Young Joe was flattened in the third round of his professional debut against unsung Paul Brown, a defeat he avenged six months later. His fifteenth opponent, Ulrich Regis from Trinidad, tragically collapsed and died after a points defeat at Shoreditch Town Hall. This weighed heavily on Joe, who was then eighteen and already carrying the responsibility of being a husband and a father.

By the time he got round to challenging Henry for his titles, Bugner had fought thirty-one times, winning twenty-nine and drawing one. He had been in the ring with only a handful of opponents of any real quality and in the case of Johnny Prescott (won points, eight rounds) and Brian London (won on a fifth-round stoppage), both his opponents were having the final fights of their careers and were way past the peak of their powers and ambition.

Bugner had not won the public over to his side because too many of his performances were pedestrian and about as exciting as watching grass grow. He so much *looked* the part with his giant frame that fans expected fireworks from him, but too often all they got was a damp squib.

Meantime, Henry's popularity was at an all-time high. In December 1970 he won the coveted BBC Sports Personality of the Year award for a second time – the first was in 1967. He was at that point the only sports star to win the trophy twice, a mark of his astonishing status in the eyes of the general public – truly a living legend, while the young Bugner had hardly made a ripple.

Henry had been able to take a good look at Bugner on his rise up the ladder and was as confident as I had ever known him when he stepped into the Wembley ring for the last fight of his career. The referee for the contest was Harry Gibbs, a stony-faced London docks worker who was generally rated the best third man in the business.

Most of the so-called experts had gone for a Bugner victory because they considered that a combination of my suspect eyes and old legs would let me down against a strong, young opponent who had a reach, height and weight advantage.

But I had trained as conscientiously for this fight as if it were a world title and I knew I was fit enough to go the full fifteen rounds, if necessary. The only concern I had was if my left elbow seized up. It had been giving me gyp for months, but I had learned to live with the pain. The specialist treatment I'd been receiving meant I was in good nick for what the press found out just before the fight was going to be my last contest.

Our battle plan was to try to keep Bugner on his back foot because he was not nearly as forceful when he had to box on the retreat. His strongest weapon was a long, solid left lead and I knew I had to block it or make him miss and then counter with my own jabs. I deliberately started at a slow pace because I wanted to have something in reserve for the later rounds when I planned to put my foot on the accelerator.

I had been in enough fifteen-round fights to know exactly how to pace myself and when and how to put on the pressure, when necessary. Hope this doesn't sound conceited, but I prided myself on being a thinking boxer and we used to plan our fights like military campaigns.

I had always been my own referee, making a mental note of how I was scoring and getting confirmation from Jim in between rounds.

It was a battle of the jabs, and for ten rounds neither Bugner nor I could have claimed we were in command. At the end of the tenth, Jim leant through the ropes and said into my ear, 'Now we've got to step up the pace. We've got to let this geezer know who's the guvnor.'

I reckon the fight was even-stevens at the two-thirds mark. In rounds eleven, twelve, thirteen and fourteen I took the fight to Bugner, beating him to the jab and doubling up my punches to the head and increasing my output at the inside exchanges. There was no doubt in my mind that I had won those four rounds and so, as I went into the fifteenth and final round – the final round of my career – I felt in my heart that Bugner had to knock me out to win.

Joe was obviously told in his corner that he was trailing, because he dug deep down into his boots and produced a grandstand finish. I met him halfway but, being charitable, I'll concede that he just shaded the round. But I was positive that I had won the fight and as the final bell rang I walked towards Harry Gibbs with my hand outstretched for him to go through the formality of raising my arm as the victor and still British, European and Empire champion.

You could have knocked me down with a featherweight when Gibbs brushed past me and went to Bugner's corner and, to Joe's utter disbelief, raised his hand. I have never been so shocked, stunned, speechless – you name it – in my life. All I could find to say was 'Cor stone me', or bleep-bleep words to that effect. It was reported that I said, 'Thought I scraped it, Harry', but I said nothing at all to him, although I'd have loved to have given him a mouthful.

My brother George had his arms wrapped around Jim Wicks, who was in the mood to give Gibbs a right-hander. 'We've been robbed, Enery,' he kept saying. 'We've been robbed.'

In a long and distinguished refereeing career, Gibbs had quite rightly gained the respect of the boxing world but on this night he had dropped a right clanger. I said exactly what I thought in my autobiography back in the 1970s, and Gibbs sued me for defamation and won his case. But I know what I know and nobody will be able to convince me otherwise.

Wembley rocked with the boos of the crowd, who agreed with my assessment of the fight. Most of the ringside reporters had me winning it and BBC commentator Harry Carpenter famously said on air, 'How can they take away a man's titles like that?' From the astonished looks on the faces of Bugner's cornermen, they also thought I'd retained my titles. I had been the victim of robbery with violence.

I've often heard it said that my going out on a sea of sympathy added to my popularity with the public. Maybe that's so, but I'd much rather have won their respect by going out as a winner and undefeated champion.

A confession here: Harry Gibbs was a family friend. He was the leader of a work gang at the London docks that included my uncle, Ted Clark, and they were close pals. For years Harry used to phone me to discuss boxing; he loved a good gossip about the fight game, and he and my dad used to meet for a drink before and after shows.

Harry always told me his conscience was clear over the Cooper/Bugner verdict and shrugged when I said I thought Henry had won by at least two rounds. 'Boxing's all about opinions,' he said. 'Henry was so loved that his fans were only seeing what they wanted to see. Joe in my eyes was a narrow but deserved winner. I called it as I saw it. In his book, Henry suggested I was less than honest. I wasn't going to stand for that, so I took him to court and won. I didn't do it for money, but just to clear my good name.'

A few years down the line I had a huge fall-out with Harry. Members of his old docks work gang were arrested for collecting things that had 'fallen off the back of a lorry' and all of them – including my Uncle Ted, Harry's big mate – were sent to prison with sentences ranging from two to four years. Gibbs was one of the few from the group that got off without charge and refused my request to give a character reference in court for my uncle, who was sent down for two years at the age of sixty-one for doing what dockers had done since time immemorial (or immoral). When I told son-of-a-Bermondsey-docker Jim Wicks, he said: 'On Harry Gibbs you can't rely.'

Jim had long gone to the great racecourse in the sky when, rather reluctantly, Henry buried the hatchet with Gibbs, agreeing to shake hands with him for charity at a fundraising boxing show at the London Hilton in the 1990s. But they never exchanged Christmas cards.

On the day of the fight, huge amounts of money were placed on Bugner to win, to the point that Jim Wicks was telephoned by his bookmaker associates to ask if Henry was carrying an injury or something. Somebody somewhere was convinced they knew the winner in advance of the fight.

Long after the Cooper contest, I represented Joe Bugner in a PR capacity. That was quite an adventure because he was as changeable as the weather: extremely likeable, but you never quite knew what mood he would be in from one hour to the next. To his face, I used to call him 'the mad Hungarian' and he would give his big friendly grin and hug me with those great bear-like arms of his. Joe had lots of charisma and charm but was often, as we in the East End affectionately described it, as silly as a box of lights.

He continually cursed winning the fight with Henry. 'I wish I'd never got the verdict against him,' he told me. 'It was as if I was the man who shot Bambi. Everybody loved Henry and the public just never forgave me for beating a legend. In the end I got so fed up with the attitude against me that I emigrated to Australia, where they always make me feel welcome.'

I put it to him that there were allegations that all was not right with the verdict. He said: 'I honestly know nothing about that. I was surprised I got the decision, not because I didn't think I had won but because Henry was and is a legend, and I didn't think they'd let me take his titles. In many ways, I wish I hadn't. Winning did me no favours and it helped make Henry an even bigger legend.'

Joe went on to lose the titles in his first defence against Jack Bodell. Yes, completely unpredictable.

In 2008, Henry and Joe were brought together by the knowledgeable Steve Bunce for the BBC programme *Inside Sport*. It was their first reunion since the controversial decision thirty-seven years earlier. Joe, who had his eighty-third and last fight at the age of forty-nine in 1999, was briefly back in London for a testimonial dinner after his Hunter Valley vineyard business had gone belly-up, leaving him bankrupt with losses of £2 million.

There was genuine warmth between the two old warriors, but they agreed to disagree on the Harry Gibbs's verdict. Both were convinced they had won – Joe not quite so convinced as Henry! In the record books there are no doubts:

Wembley Arena, 16 March 1971: Joe Bugner won points 15.

As Henry said when he returned to the dressing-room after the fight: 'That's it. That's me lot.'

A great career was over. A remarkable new career was about to begin.

ROUND 13

THE CELEBRITY CIRCUIT

When most champions step off the sporting stage, they gradually drop out of the spotlight. Not Henry. His popularity increased to the point where he was rivalling even the Queen Mother as Britain's best-loved personality. The fact that he had a huge framed photograph of himself and the Queen Mum on the wall at the Cooper home proved that he was an unashamed royalist.

Henry was so lucky to have found Jim Wicks to manage his boxing career. He was equally lucky to have found the perfect person to handle his business affairs during a time when he was the most sought-after ex-sportsman in the land. For more than forty years he was guided through the minefield of media, endorsement, advertising, speech-making and corporate appearances by the esteemed showbusiness agent Johnnie Riscoe, who was later joined by his bubbly, energetic and impeccably organised daughter, Patsy Martin.

Bad agents can quickly wreck a celebrity's reputation by choosing the wrong products to advertise, or by placing stories that can damage rather than develop their client's standing and impair rather than improve the image. Johnnie and Patsy always got it just right, from the amusing Brut 'Splash It All Over' campaign, through the Shredded Wheat, Plax, Crown Paint and Pizza Hut promotions, and into his senior years as the affable advocate for the Flu Jab ('Don't get knocked out by flu, get your jab in first'). They also booked Henry's many television appearances, including for what was then the pioneering quiz programme *A Question of Sport*, with David Vine as the presenter and rugby great Cliff Morgan as the rival team captain.

'Between us,' Patsy told me, 'Dad and I were proud to represent Henry for around forty-three years. He was always a joy to handle, a man of great warmth and also integrity. His genial personality, particularly when combined with that of my dear friend Albina, was just infectious. Everybody, but everybody, loved Henry. We were responsible for booking him for hundreds – and I do mean hundreds – of after-dinner speeches, personal appearances, book and television and radio work. And so much of it was done for charity, with Henry refusing a fee and always insisting on driving himself to and from the event and not charging expenses. It was quite astonishing the way he put himself out to help others. There will never be another Henry. He was an agent's dream, and I am so privileged to have known him and to have represented him. Henry was a champion, in and out of the ring.'

Henry and Johnnie Riscoe had something other than business helping to cement their friendship – the game of golf. They were both fairway fanatics and a celebrity golf tournament could not start until Henry arrived at the tee, usually in the company of showbusiness buddies like Jimmy Tarbuck, Terry Wogan, Ronnie Corbett, Bruce Forsyth, Michael Parkinson, Frank Carson, Russ Abbot and Kenny Lynch. The golfing equivalent of the Rat Pack, they helped raise millions of pounds for charity in scores of fundraising pro-am golf tournaments.

Jim Wicks and Johnnie Riscoe were two of the most important people in my life. Jim guided me through my boxing career as carefully and as conscientiously as if he was my dad. Then Johnnie, and his darling daughter Patsy, looked after me outside the ring with loving care; I was a very lucky boy. Later on I had the unforgettable Fleet Street agency powerhouse Reg Hayter organising book and newspaper deals for me and then Terry Baker, a lively entrepreneur from down in Dorset, set up a series of road shows. But, no question, it was Johnnie Riscoe and Patsy who did most to keep me in the public eye and with a nice few earners along the way.

It was Johnnie who kept encouraging me to concentrate on my golf because he knew it would give me the perfect outlet for my energy once the daily grind of training was suddenly over. I was chuffed to be made executive chairman of the Variety Club of Great Britain Golfing Society, which was brilliantly run by Johnnie and Patsy. Through that I made life-long friends with scores of showbiz people including, of course, Tarby, Terry Wogan, Ronnie Corbett, Bruce Forsyth and the like. You can imagine the stick I've had to take playing with that lot, particularly when I've been hooking the ball off the tee. Tarby would say things like, 'Our Enery's 'Ammer is back – everybody duck!'

I was particularly proud to host the annual Henry Cooper Golfing Classic at Muswell Hill, with all proceeds going to the Ex-Boxers' Association. A lot of the old fighters were not as lucky as me and many of them were on their uppers. It was great to have the opportunity to raise a few bob to help them.

People ask me if I've any regrets and I have to say the only one is that I didn't get more consistent on the golf course. One day I could play like a single handicapper, the next like a complete rabbit. I had a slice that Hovis could not have bettered and I've spent more time in bunkers than Hitler. It's the most frustrating game ever invented, and I've loved every minute of playing, even on the bad days. I spent so much time at the London Golf Club, near Brands Hatch, that it became like a second home and Albina used to say I should have my bed there. But she was as good as gold about all the time I spent on the course – I suppose it kept me from getting under her feet.

Cliff Morgan and I had a ball on *A Question of Sport* and to think we got paid for it. He was something of an intellectual, while I used to crash through the grammar gears and dropping aitches all over the place. But it worked, and we had a good chemistry. Back then my memory was working and I had quite a good knowledge of sports history and the personalities of the day. I can remember the first show as if it was yesterday. Actually it was 1970 and the team guests were George Best, the lovely Lillian Board, England cricket captain Ray Illingworth and football legend Tom Finney. Best and Finney on the same show, arguably the two greatest ever British footballers.

What viewers didn't know is that those early shows were filmed in an old Manchester church that had been converted and we used to shoot the programmes on a Sunday in what used to be the nave. Dear old David Vine used to pretend he was a vicar and would give a sham sermon to the audience just to get them warmed up: 'Dearly beloved, we're gathered here today', all that sort of stuff, and he'd add, 'During our first hymn, Cliff Morgan and Henry Cooper will pass among you with the collecting box: please give generously.' Lovely days.

But the most fun I had in front of a camera was when I was making the 'Splash It All Over' ads for Brut, with Kevin Keegan and Barry Sheene putting some youth into the commercials. They were a great couple of characters and the hardest job the director had was trying to stop us laughing so they could shoot the scripted bits. Barry was a real rascal and would deliberately try to make me corpse when I was saying my lines. He had so much metal holding him together after a couple of serious crashes that he could have played the Six Million Dollar Man for real. When he used to arrive on the set he would say to the crew, 'If any of you've got magnets, please leave them outside, otherwise you're going to find yourself drawn to me and we could have some embarrassing moments.'

I remember a solo commercial I did for Brut, in which I was singing Gershwin's 'Summertime' in the bath. We must have shot it thirty times and then the director settled on the first take. I got to hate that bloody song! The adverts were amazingly popular and for years I couldn't go anywhere without somebody shouting, 'Splash it all over, Enery!' Tell you what, it was a much better way of making a crust than getting your nose bashed in.

Yes, it was sweet smell of success time. Free from the disciplines of boxing, Henry discovered a taste for wine and champagne, though never over-indulging. For the first time in his life he started smoking to the point that in 1984 he was named Pipe Smoker of the Year, which he described as 'another nice little earner' because he was paid by the tobacco company for the publicity shots.

★ ★ ★

Henry had a wonderful life with more adventures, rich experiences and entertainment than half a dozen other people have had between them. Something I have not touched on in this maze of a memoir is his insistence on a good family holiday. Here, he is remembering some of his happiest days, reminiscing about holidays, the good and the bad. You can warm your hands on his memories:

We were very big on holidays, Albina and me. You have to remember that we were both from poor backgrounds, so didn't get away much when we were kids. In fact the only holidays George, Bernard and I had were when Mum and Dad used to take us down to Margate to stay with my Auntie Mary and Uncle Jim.

I remember the donkey-walks man, a wizened little guy who wore a bowler hat and big overcoat regardless of the weather. He looked, dare I say, donkey's years old and he used to let us lead his docile animals from the Margate Dreamland amusement park to the beach. We'd make a couple of bob, then go and spend it on sweets and in Dreamland, which back then was one of the biggest amusement parks in the country. George and I used to love going on the big dipper and would bash each other all over the shop on the bumper cars.

The first holiday Albina and I went on – not counting our honeymoon – was a disaster. We went on our first and last cruise. Albina had never even been on a boat before, so I guess I was a bit unwise to book a four-week tour of the French West Indies. We went on a French cruiser, *L'Antilles*, which I'd been told was one of the most luxurious ships afloat. Almost as soon as my lovely Albina stepped aboard this floating palace she complained of feeling queasy – and I don't think her confidence was improved when she saw the crew nailing all the furniture to the deck. They'd had a warning of an approaching storm, but didn't share the information with us.

Suddenly, in the middle of our first night on board, the storm struck and we were thrown from our beds as the ship started to rock and roll. For the next five days poor Albina was as sick as a dog, with a green face. Desperate for dry land, we finally escaped and booked into a hotel that didn't move. Albina had to admit to being the worst sailor ever and just looking at the water used to make her feel seasick. There were times when we would have to make the short hop across the Channel and the captain of the ferry used to let her lie down in his cabin. I was offered dozens of free cruises, with me in a sort of meeting and greeting role, but I turned them all down. I wasn't going anywhere without my Albina.

When Henry Marco and John Pietro were growing up we had some super holidays at the Hotel Dona Filipa, on the Algarve. It is right beside both the Vale do Lobo golf course and the sea, so all the family were happy. The boys would spend their days on the beach, Albina sunbathed and I played golf. Paradise! I often used to drive down through Europe and the best drive was in my Jensen Interceptor, one of the most attractive cars I ever owned – I used to really get my foot down with it. Thank goodness Albina didn't suffer carsickness.

Whenever Albina and I decided on a holiday, I used to get her mad by insisting there had to be a golf course view from the hotel window. Nothing better than to be able to see a golf course from the bedroom when you get up first thing in the morning.

I've stayed at some fantastic courses, but Gleneagles up in Scotland and one of the venues for the British Open has to be the best. There's no place on earth quite like it. The bathrooms are as big as the bedrooms – and they had huge baths in which even I could lie stretched out. In most hotel baths I have my knees up under my chin, but this was sheer luxury.

We've made some wonderful friends playing golf there, including Bob Hope and Bing Crosby, when we took part in a pro-am. They were a bundle of laughs, and to make the break at Gleneagles even better, our bill was paid by the tournament organisers.

One of our most memorable holidays was a safari in Kenya. We stayed at Treetops, in the heart of the jungle. This was where Princess Elizabeth was staying in 1952 when she learned of her father's death and that she was the new monarch. I recall that our room had a trunk growing up through the middle of it. Albina was concerned that a monkey or something might climb up it in the middle of the night, but I told her that we were the only wild animals there.

We went on that holiday with our good friends Bobby Charlton and his wife Norma. Our safari guide said: 'If there's a kill, do you want to see it?' It sounded a bit gruesome but we agreed we were up for it, Albina and Norma with some trepidation. We got a call at 4 a.m. and drove deep into the bush. There, just a few yards in front of us, was a big huddle of about fifteen or more bloodied lions. They'd just killed a buffalo and were sleeping it off. We had just missed the massacre, thank goodness. I suppose that's nature, but I'd seen enough blood in boxing, thank you very much.

Gradually the lions started to wake up, one by one, in what could have been a scene from *The Jungle Book* and the young lionesses kissed and nuzzled their mother before making their way down to the water. It was the most amazing sight. Bobby was banging off right, left and centre with his camera, which was just as well as I – big dummy – had left our camera in the hotel.

Albina is at her most relaxed and happy when we visit Boccacci, the village near Parma in northern Italy where she grew up. It feels like a second home to me, yet it's very different to the Italy I used to visit with George at the end of each boxing season. Then, we'd stay in a top hotel, noshing first-class food in stunning surroundings. But on my honeymoon I was introduced to another side of Italy and spent two weeks in a house without electricity, gas or running water. We managed to slip in a bit of luxury, too, by going to Diano Marino on the Italian Riviera for a wonderful week alone.

It was quite an eye-opener going to Boccacci for the first time. The terrain on the way to the village in the foothills of the Apennine mountain range was so rugged that we had to leave the car about two miles away, load our luggage onto a wooden sleigh and walk behind the two cows that pulled it along. I asked myself several times what I was doing trudging up a mountain in ninety-degree heat. But once we got there, the food and the warm welcome from Albina's family made it all worthwhile.

If I had to choose my favourite place, it's Penina on the Algarve. That's where I used to hold my annual golf classic tournament, in partnership with the comedian Mike Reid, on a course designed by the legendary Sir Henry Cotton. It was supposed to be 'work', but they were the best holidays we could ever imagine. And what made it so satisfying is that we raised thousands of pounds for deserving causes. All that and sunshine too. It doesn't get better than that.

Retirement wasn't all fun and laughter, though. In 1991 a huge black cloud dropped on the Coopers, when much of the fortune Henry had worked so hard to earn was wiped out in the infamous Lloyd's Names scandal that followed in the wake of the 1987 stock market crash.

Henry had been an underwriting syndicate member since hanging up his gloves after being advised to invest his money by his good friend, insurance broker Charles St George. He got some nice little tickles from it, but unbeknown to its thousands of members, Lloyd's was in huge financial trouble. When the crash came, it meant all those who had committed themselves to unlimited liability were responsible for the colossal Lloyd's debts.

Many members had to sell their prize assets, including their houses, to meet the sudden king-size debt. It looked as if the Coopers were going to lose the superb six-bedroom home they had moved to in an exclusive part of Hendon. When the story broke, Jimmy Tarbuck was one of the first on the phone offering financial help. Henry was deeply moved by the gesture from a true friend, but politely refused. He was on the canvas and was going to get himself up.

Henry decided the only way out of the crisis was to sell the three Lonsdale Belts he had won, literally with blood, sweat and a few tears.

That was the worst and most worrying period of our lives. The shock that a company like Lloyd's could go under was just beyond belief. Albina was wonderful and kept her nerve better than me; thanks to her we both adopted the attitude that 'what's meant to be, will be'. We were lucky that we had our faith to keep us strong; there were a lot worse off than us.

We had been through a similar thing with the greengrocer's shop, but this was a thousand times worse. It looked as if we were going to lose our beautiful house for a while, but once I got my head around it I decided the Belts would have to go. I was hoping to pass them on to Henry Marco and John Pietro, for them to ultimately pass on to their children. But it wasn't meant to be.

A lot of good people were wiped out by the Lloyd's crash, so we were more fortunate than most in that we had the Belts to help get us out of trouble. The auctioneers reckoned they would fetch a hundred grand, but I stupidly allowed myself to be talked into putting them up for auction in Kent, when it was obvious the big punters were in London. They went for £42,000, which was very disappointing, but at least it got us off the hook. And I don't mean that as anything of a pun: this was no laughing matter.

Albina, bless her, convinced me that it was time to let the house go. Our boys had both got married, so we were rattling around. We downsized to a nice coach house in a lovely part of Kent and found real happiness and contentment there.

There are a lot of things I could say about that Lloyd's business but

I'm best off keeping my mouth shut. We got away lightly compared to some. People who had gone into it thinking it was as safe as the Bank of England lost everything they had. They were sucked into it by grasping sales people, who knew it could all go to pot. It was fraudulent and outrageous. A lot of victims tried to fight Lloyd's in court, but I couldn't be bothered with all that. As far as I was concerned, it was blood under the bridge.

The greengrocer's, the City. What did I know about them? I had been taken to the cleaners in worlds that were foreign to me. The advice I always pass on to my boys is that if you're going to risk any money, only do it in areas that you know. There are a lot of sharks out there and they had bitten me where it hurts. In the wallet.

As if following a knockout defeat in the boxing ring, Henry picked himself up, dusted himself off and got on with his life, increasing his celebrity appearance work and after-dinner speeches. His self-assessment of his speeches: 'I'm not exactly Oscar Wilde but I just try to be myself and tell them a few inside stories and answer their questions. No good worrying about me grammar. Should have done that at school! My speeches seem to go down well, yeah.'

He somehow managed to give even more of his energy to helping those in need. I have been around sportsmen all my working life – fifty-five years and counting – and have known few who could match his spirit of generosity. It was almost as if supporting those down on their luck was a calling. The time he gave to boosting worthy causes was just unbelievable and among his favourite charities was the Grand Order of Water Rats, which has a huge membership of major showbusiness luminaries. He had a year as King Rat, with the Duke of Edinburgh among his loyal servants.

Henry's charity work, particularly on behalf of underprivileged children, was recognised by the Pope, who bestowed upon him the Papal Knighthood of St Gregory. Cardinal Basil Hume, a self-confessed boxing fan, presented it to Henry in a moving ceremony in Westminster Cathedral, with Albina in tears of joy and pride.

Another knighthood was on its way, and this time it would mean an extra title in the Cooper household: Lady Albina Cooper, which was appropriate for everybody's favourite lady.

ARISE SIR HENRY

The New Millennium dawned with the proudest day of Henry's life. In the New Year's Honours List for 2000 it was announced that he was to be knighted by the Queen. The boy from the Bellingham council estate had come a long, long way.

He was the first boxer ever knighted, the honour being given for his services to boxing coupled with his extraordinary efforts in fundraising charity work. As he knelt before the Queen for the ancient shoulder-touching sword ceremony, Henry admitted to mixed emotions:

> I was busting with pride, but just wished my old mum and dad and dear old Jim Wicks had been there to share the moment. We were just ordinary people, and here I was kneeling before the Queen of England and being told, 'Arise Sir Henry'. Blimey, that was something very, very special.
>
> You can imagine the joy and the laughs Albina and I had when I was first invited to become a knight. Sir Henry and Lady Albina Cooper. Me from the Bellingham council estate, Albina from peasant farming stock. Albina kept on saying how proud she was of me, but I

was lucky to be able to share it with her. Henry Marco and John Pietro were, well, as pleased as punch.

What gave me tremendous satisfaction is that I got the knighthood as much for my charity work as my boxing. I don't want this to sound over the top, but I've always wanted to try to give something back. I've had a great life and have been very fortunate to be always surrounded by a loving family and loyal friends so I am entitled to feel grateful and help those who have not had my good luck.

I felt very humbled by the knighthood and was determined to make it work for me in my appearances for charity. It meant I had a little more pulling power for fundraising and I started to work more for wonderful organisations like the Lord's Taverners and the Prince's Trust. In fact, one of the first things I got was an invitation from Prince Charles to attend his Night of Knights dinner at the Royal Lancaster Hotel in aid of his Trust. I was delighted to be in the company of other sporting knights like Sir Bobby Charlton, Sir Roger Bannister and Sir Gary Sobers, all idols of mine from way back.

If my knighthood had come a few months earlier I would have had to hobble towards the Queen! I had managed to get bitten on my ankle by a snake – an adder – while playing golf on a course in Buckinghamshire. I thought nothing of it until several weeks later, when the ankle suddenly blew up to three times its usual size. I was in agony and had to have all sorts of medication and treatment. That bloody adder had apparently planted eggs in my ankle. Jimmy Tarbuck said I should have conceded the hole for 'adding' to my score. It was more painful than anything I had known in boxing.

The knighthood was universally acclaimed and the Cooper home inundated with congratulatory messages from around the world; it took Lady Albina Cooper and Patsy Martin weeks to reply to them all. Muhammad Ali ordered a fax to be sent by one of his entourage, who helped him through times of poor health: 'Guess this makes YOU the greatest, Sir Henry.'

Now in his sixty-seventh year, Henry showed no signs of relaxing his relentless drive to raise money for good causes. If anything, the knighthood increased the demands on his time and energy. He was still a crowd-puller on the commercial front and his 'Flu Jab' TV and poster campaign was responsible for hundreds of thousands of senior citizens signing up for the NHS battle against influenza.

The older he got, the more Henry started to distance himself from boxing. He used to put himself in the front line in defence of the sport and once had a headline-hitting exchange with Baroness Edith Summerskill, who for many years was the leading spokesperson for abolitionists who wanted the sport banned.

They came face to face in a live (and lively) debate on television and the Baroness, to underscore the point that punches can damage, leaned forward and said: 'Mr Cooper, have you looked in the mirror and seen the state of your nose?'

Henry threw an instant verbal counter punch with all the sweet timing of his favourite left hook: 'Well, have you had a butcher's at yours, Baroness? Boxing's my excuse. What's yours?'

It was a full minute before the audience stopped laughing and they could resume the debate and from that moment on there was only one winner.

Henry – *Sir* Henry – had taken over the Barrington Dalby role as inter-round summariser on BBC radio's coverage of boxing, but he eventually had to give it up because he could no longer maintain the pretence that he was enjoying the job. He was wise enough to recognise he was becoming the Victor Meldrew of boxing commentaries, moaning as much about the fight game as Freddie Trueman was about modern cricket on *Test Match Special*. His final broadcast was the night Frank Bruno took the WBC world heavyweight title from Oliver McCall at Wembley. Henry had never been a fan of Bruno the boxer, much as he liked him as Bruno the man; his opinion was that Bruno was a stiff, manufactured fighter rather than a relaxed natural one and that Oliver McCall, from whom Bruno took the title, was one of the most mediocre champions he had ever seen.

I put the words into Bruno's mouth for much of his career as his spin-doctor and it led to my one sharp exchange with Henry, after I'd fed Frank a line about the old heavyweights not being able to live with the modern champions because they were little more than cruiserweights. Henry pulled me up on it and told me: 'You're putting words into the mouth of a dummy.'

Good luck to Frank. He's always been a dedicated professional and a good advertisement for how boxing can help change your life for the better. But if this is the standard of world championship boxing, I want no part of it. The game's gone.

Suppose I can be accused of living in the past, but it's become a farce. It is taking boxers longer to make their ring entrance than it is to fight. They're coming up with all sorts of stupid gimmicks, like approaching the ring on a motorbike or a magic carpet, or through so much smoke that it's like peering through one of those old London smogs.

I've always tried to be true to myself, and I found that I was telling porkies about boxers who would not have lived with the best of my time. Sorry to do the 'in my day' bit, but we used to have just eight world champions, one for each weight. Now there are something like eighty boxers claiming to be world champion, with four or five different alphabet versions of their title.

You will never hear me knock boxing. It has given me a good life and I enjoyed nearly every second of my career except when the old ref was counting over me. But the way it's going, I can't see the public being interested in it for much longer. These days kids are fighting for a world title after fewer than a dozen fights. It's a nonsense. They have not learned their craft. Good luck to 'em, but I'm not going to sit at the mic and tell any more lies. The standard today is – apart from for a handful of exceptional fighters – just appalling.

As he moved into the autumn of his years, Henry was not blessed with the best of health. He suffered aggravating deafness, painful bouts of arthritis and gout – despite having been only a moderate drinker – and he had to have an operation on the left hand that had served him so well as a plasterer and a puncher. While hosting his annual Henry Cooper Golfing Classic at Muswell Hill in July 2006, he got the fright of his life when he suddenly struggled to breathe. Whipped off to hospital, he had a pacemaker fitted to control his heartbeat.

Just a month later, Henry and Albina drove all the way down to Dorset to join me in saying a final, fond farewell to Eileen, my lovely wife of forty-five years. What a man to make that effort so soon after such a shock to his system – there's the true Henry Cooper for you. Jimmy Greaves was also at the funeral and Henry greeted him like a long-lost brother. 'How you keeping, Jim?' he said. 'Haven't seen you for yonks.'

Greavsie replied: 'You silly sod, we did a show together last week.' That was when we started to worry about Henry and his physical condition.

We were all concerned about his increasing frailty, none of us dreaming that it was the effervescent Albina who needed the attention. In the summer of 2008, the day after Henry had been diagnosed with having a heart defect, 71-year-old Albina died suddenly of a heart attack at home, almost certainly brought on by constant worrying about her beloved husband's health.

From then on, Henry and I could hardly talk to each other without being choked up over the loss of our wives, our best friends.

We were both so lucky to find such wonderful wives. When Albina and I were at Eileen's funeral, we wondered how you were going to be able to cope. Well, now I've got the same challenge.

I am lost without her. She looked after me hand and foot, was my ears and my eyes. To be honest, I am really struggling. I've got a candle in front of my favourite photograph of her and I light it every night in her memory. I take her ashes in an urn with me if ever I am staying somewhere overnight. I know that sounds morbid, but it just sort of keeps me in touch

She'll tell me off for being so soppy, but I just don't know how I'm going to manage without her. I've got the two boys and their wives and my grandchildren, and they are all being very supportive. Henry, in particular, is being a rock for me. He has taken over from Albina in getting me organised and ferrying me to and from my various appointments, but life's just not the same anymore. Always thought I'd go first. I'm in shock; just can't take it in.

Henry and I last met up at Harry Carpenter's memorial service at St Bride's Church, off Fleet Street. Henry Junior was in charge of him and flitting around in the same conscientious and caring way that his mother had for so many years as Henry's right (and left) hand. I was shocked at how frail and feeble the old champion looked but I got the same cheerful 'Watchyer, Norm!' greeting and big smile he had given me when we first met at the Thomas a Becket gymnasium fifty-two years earlier. That day at St Bride's, I mourned the passing of Harry Carpenter and worried about my friend Sir Henry Cooper.

To compound his desolation, Henry's inseparable twin brother George passed on in the spring of 2010 after a long debilitating illness that had confined him to home for many months.

For the one and only time, Henry – *Sir* Henry – was ready to throw in the towel.

THE FINAL BELL

Death came in the afternoon of May Day 2011 and I know dear Henry would not object to me making as light of it as I can. For many years we had ribbed each other over his support of Arsenal and mine for bitter rivals Tottenham. How poignant, then, that he should die while watching his beloved Arsenal play Manchester United on television.

Our hero had been living for several months at Henry Marco's home in Oxted, Surrey, being nursed through what his loving son knew would be his final days. His dad had been diagnosed with a worsening defective heart in January 2010 and his life expectancy was given as no more than fifteen months.

He was sitting in an armchair, dozing in and out of the match, and Henry Junior went into the kitchen to get him a snack. 'When I returned, Dad was slumped in the chair,' Henry said. 'I knew straight away that he'd gone. It was, thank God, quick and painless. The last thing he said to me was, "What's the score?"' Aaron Ramsey had scored a winning goal for Arsenal so that would have pleased Aitch.

While his passing was desperately sad, it was not a major shock to those who knew him well. We were all of the opinion that he had lost the will to live the moment of the passing of his precious Albina, followed soon afterwards by the departure of George.

He died just about the same time as Bin Laden was killed in the raid in Pakistan, so suddenly the newspapers and television programmes were awash with news of the assassination. But space was also found to give Henry the send-off he deserved, and the response to his passing was staggering. This was for an ex-boxer who had not fought for forty years.

Henry Marco and John Pietro were buried under an avalanche of sympathy messages and tributes from all around the world. 'The world has lost a true gentleman' was the message from Muhammad Ali, just one of the many accolades compiled in the 'Homage to a Hero' section later in this book.

★ ★ ★

The sun came out for Sir Henry on his final journey. Hundreds of fans paid their last respects to our hero, lining the leafy streets of Oxted in Surrey as the cortège – Sir Henry's coffin draped with the Union Jack and on top a red wreath in the shape of a boxing glove and 'Our Enery' spelt out in white chrysanthemums – slowly passed by on its way to the funeral service in Tonbridge, Kent, eighteen miles away. The family wisely decided on a private thanksgiving service for Henry because a public funeral would have brought Tonbridge to a standstill. Sir Henry, for all his fabled fame, was not a man who enjoyed fuss.

The Cooper family – Henry Marco, John Pietro, their wives, children, aunts, uncles and cousins – were all just about cried out,

Henry's death coming when the tears had hardly dried for the passing of Albina and George. The emotionally charged service was conducted by Father Tom McElhone at the Corpus Christi Church, sunshine sending shimmering shafts of rainbow light through the beautiful stained-glass windows. There was a staggering turnout, with celebrities and sporting superstars mixed in with family and close friends. Sitting immediately to the right of me were Sir Bruce Forsyth and Cliff Morgan; to my left, Sir Terry Wogan, Peter Alliss, Lawrie McMenemy, goalkeeping legend Pat Jennings and the ever-faithful Patsy Martin; in the pew behind, Barry McGuigan, Des Lynam and major sportswriters Hugh McIlvanney and Colin Hart; over there, Sir Bobby Charlton, Kenny Lynch, Kevin Keegan and Sir Trevor Brooking; behind, Russ Abbot, former Arsenal chief executive Ken Friar, Henry's old opponent Billy Walker, promoter Ron Gray, entrepreneurs Terry and Freda Baker, and in front, Henry's long-time golfing pal, Jimmy Tarbuck.

It was Jimmy who spoke for us all in a suitably respectful but amusing eulogy, simply yet so accurately calling Henry 'a very, very nice man'. Tarby brought laughter to go with the tears when he told how he was with a group of celebrities at a golf tournament in Devon when, at his bidding, everybody at their hotel dining table stood up and started singing 'Happy Birthday' to Henry, who sat looking blank because it was not his birthday. In no time, bottles of champagne began arriving at the table from fellow guests. 'See, Aitch,' Jimmy told Henry, 'now you *feel* as if it's your birthday!'

Jimmy then got the tear ducts working as he added: 'Henry was, in the words of his Cockney fans, a real diamond geezer. To be born a gentleman, as he was, is an accident; but to die one is a real achievement. Henry has left us to be with his lover, best friend and organiser, Albina.'

Henry Marco and John Pietro gave their idolised dad the dignified send-off he deserved. The simple yet reverential Requiem Mass reflected Henry's devout Roman Catholic faith. He was borne in to 'Amazing Grace' before Henry Marco welcomed the congregation ahead of the singing of 'Abide With Me'.

There were readings by Neal and Daryl Cooper and the bidding prayers were led by Barbara Cooper. Father Nolan gave the Gospel acclamation; he had married Henry and Albina fifty years earlier and guided Aitch through his conversion to Roman Catholicism. 'Henry will be remembered for his feats in the boxing ring,' said Father Nolan, 'but equally for being an exemplary human being who was always looking to help others less fortunate than himself.'

Other hymns included Henry's personal favourites 'Guide Me O Thou Great Redeemer', 'Ave Maria' and 'Jerusalem'. The sword never slept in Henry's hand and he brought joy to England's green and pleasant land.

The exit music had everybody half crying and half laughing. It was a recording that Henry – not the greatest singer – had made in the 1970s of an old Cockney song, 'Knock Me Down With A Feather', with a chorus that could have been dedicated to Albina:

> Well, you can knock me down with a feather,
> So long as we're always together,
> I'll never fall out of love with you…

As we walked out into the afternoon sunlight behind Henry's coffin, there was an outbreak of polite, respectful applause from hundreds of members of the general public, who had found their way through the police cordon surrounding the roads leading to the church.

The immediate family went on to the crematorium for a private final service, with Henry's ashes later being mixed with those of Albina.

Meanwhile, the rest of us headed for the wake at Henry's second home, the London Golf Club near Brands Hatch, where everybody paid homage to Sir Henry Cooper, A Hero for All Time.

HOMAGE TO A HERO

And so I reach the end of my journey through Henry Cooper's life and times. It was only the day before yesterday that he first greeted me with what was to become that famous smile, a crushing handshake that was semaphore for sincerity and the warmly delivered: 'Watchyer, Norm'.

No, my mind is playing tricks. It was actually fifty-three years ago, and he greeted me in exactly the same way the last time we met, at Harry Carpenter's memorial service in St Bride's Church in Fleet Street.

The adventure he had experienced between those two greetings was a rollercoaster – mainly ups, occasional downs, never, ever dull and always with optimism, expectation and faith as travelling companions.

For Henry, the peak was not the punch that famously knocked down Cassius Clay. No, the peak by far was meeting and falling in love with the gorgeous, the sensitive, the affectionate Albina, his strength and his shield, the love of his life.

I am deeply grateful and honoured that their sons, Henry Marco and John Pietro, have given their blessing for this book and I hope

I have provided at least a flavour of the qualities and experiences that made their father a Hero for All Time.

If you have been at all moved by the story and share with me the admiration and respect for all that Henry did for charity, please join me in making a donation, no matter how small, to the Sir Henry Cooper Charity Fund, so that we can help carry on the work that Our Enery performed with all his energy and total sincerity.

Contact me by email at henry@normangillerbooks.co.uk for full details of how you can contribute, or make direct payments to the Sir Henry Cooper Charity Fund, Lloyds TSB Bank, account number 22643860, sort code: 30-97-49.

To make this a complete portrait of our hero, I want to capture how Sir Henry was revered and respected throughout the twin worlds of sport and showbusiness in which he moved so comfortably and graciously. Tributes following his passing poured in on a tide of tears and his sons, Henry Marco and John Pietro, and their wives worked overtime to respond to as many as possible.

Most of the following accolades I have gathered myself; others have been passed on by the family and old Fleet Street colleagues. A parade of knights from sport and showbusiness queued to pay their respects and to talk from the heart about our hero.

MUHAMMAD ALI:

I am at a loss for words over the death of my dear friend Henry Cooper. I was not aware he was ill and so his passing came as a huge shock. I looked on him not as a former opponent but as a great friend. I visited with him two summers ago during a brief visit to Windsor, as part of the Equestrian Games being held there. He was in good humour and looked quite fit.

Henry always had a smile for me, a warm and embracing smile. We met many times after our two contests, in both of which he gave me lots of problems, including that punch that shook up my ancestors in Africa. If he had not cut so easily, he would have been an even more successful boxer.

It was always a pleasure being in Henry's company. I will miss my old friend. He was a great fighter and a gentleman, in and out of the ring. My family and I extend our heartfelt sympathies to his family and loved ones. He will be greatly missed.

SIR BOBBY CHARLTON:

We knew Henry was unwell, but it still came as a sad surprise when Norma and I heard he had died. From the moment he lost Albina, we knew he was in trouble. She was his rock and shield.

Henry and I knew each other throughout our sporting careers and became good friends after we had both retired. Norma and Albina got on famously. He was always unassuming, and comfortable to be with and his smile lit up the room. For a man who was so violent inside the ring, he was a real gentle giant away from boxing. It was difficult to imagine that this was the same person who had knocked down Cassius Clay.

He loved his football and told me that if he had not taken up boxing he might have had a career as a goalkeeper. Henry would certainly have filled a lot of the goal with that big frame of his. He was an Arsenal supporter, of course, and I used to tell him it was the wrong colour red. His fame transcended sport, and he was a wonderful role model for any young people looking for an example of how to conduct themselves both in and out of their sport. The work he did for charity captured the man. He was always trying to help others. He will be hugely missed, but always warmly remembered.

SIR TERRY WOGAN:

We will never see another Henry. They threw away the mould. He was not only a great champion of boxing, but a champion of human beings. His work for charity, much of it done quietly and out of the public eye, was quite extraordinary. For all his achievements and fame, he managed to stay that same affable, unassuming Henry, with whom the British public have had a long love affair. Now he is reunited with his beloved Albina.

He truly measured up to the image of a great sporting hero, meeting those two impostors triumph and disaster and treating them both the same. The final bell has tolled, but he will live on in the memory.

SIR MICHAEL PARKINSON:

I think a measure of Henry is that I have never known anybody who did not like him, even his former opponents. My old chat show adversary Muhammad Ali was full of praise for him, as a boxer but more so as a man. He was generous with his time, was kind, and could be very humorous. If Henry was in your company you could bet there would soon be laughter.

He was the best kind of athlete, the best kind of boxer; he wasn't boastful, he was genuinely modest and a gentleman. I consider him in the same way as I do Bobby Charlton – the two of them represent something which I think has gone out of sport rather, *that* kind of hero. His work for many charities was just astounding. He never allowed fame to change him and was and always will be Our Enery.

SIR BRUCE FORSYTH:

I always followed Henry's boxing career and got to know him well through our mutual love for golf. He gave everything he had to everything he did, whether it was in the boxing ring or working for charities. What a role model for sportsmen. He showed by example how to lead a life in and out of the sports arena. I felt privileged to know him and to call him a friend. He will be greatly missed but never forgotten. He is a sporting legend.

SIR TREVOR BROOKING:

Henry was without question one of the most loved people in the country, whether you knew anything about sport or not. He made a name for himself in the world of boxing, but his fame transcended anything he did in the ring because of the way he conducted himself away from his sport. Henry always had time for people and his fund-raising for charities was a thing of legend.

He loved football and in particular Arsenal, and it was very moving to hear that he passed away while watching the Gunners play Manchester United on television. A big, bright light has gone out on the sporting stage.

SIR DAVID FROST:

I recall being at a Best of British Millennium Lunch hosted by the Queen. Henry was there, along with, among many others: Dame Vera Lynn, Roger Bannister, and Bobby Charlton. That's the sort of bracket Henry can be counted in. A real national treasure. The last time I saw him was in 2008 at a Michael Parkinson book launch. He had lost his wonderful wife not long before, and was looking weary. But it still came as a shock to hear of his passing. He was a wonderful ambassador for the Best of British.

SIR ROGER BANNISTER:

Henry and I attended many events together over the last fifty or more years. We go back a long way, because we were both members of the 1952 Olympic team in Helsinki. I always found him a very affable and modest man, and it was hard to imagine him trying to hurt an opponent in the ring. I am deeply saddened to hear of his passing, and British sport has lost a man who set high standards of sportsmanship and dedication.

SIR IAN BOTHAM:

Henry and I had *A Question of Sport* in common, and I followed him as a team captain. He and Cliff Morgan set high standards when the show was first launched. I have met him many times on the charity and after-dinner speaking circuit and never found him anything less than cheerful and good company. He was a legend in boxing, and even people who know nothing about boxing knew of Henry and his 'Ammer. He was one of the most popular British sportsmen of any time, and will be greatly missed.

JIMMY TARBUCK:

It was an honour to give the eulogy for dear old Henry – a great responsibility, because I was speaking on behalf of the nation about a man who was a national treasure.

We loved him on the celebrity golf circuit because he was such good company: never the greatest golfer, but always dreaming of being the best. Pity about his hook! He could take a joke and a lot of leg-pulling went on, but he never once lost that genial, gentle giant image. I never saw him turn down a request for an autograph, and he was always last to leave our fundraising tournaments because he was giving so much time to the public. Yes, a nice man. A very nice man.

RONNIE CORBETT:

The last time we were all together with Henry was for Tarby's Golden Wedding in Mayfair, and he was still mourning the loss of his wonderful wife, Albina. I prefer to think of him as the cheerful and ebullient man at the centre of so many of our golfing get-togethers. He loved his golf, particularly when he knew that by playing he was helping a charity raise money for a good cause. Henry was a huge favourite of the galleries and he always had a large following watching him hook his way around the course. We used to joke that he played more like Gladys Cooper, and he took it all in good spirit. He truly was one of a kind, and a pleasant, ultra-polite man that you just could not imagine hammering opponents to the canvas. Thanks for the memories, Henry.

RUSS ABBOT:

Henry was simply the Best of British. We were often together doing our bit at things like Variety Club events and particularly at golf tournaments, and Henry lit up the fairway – and sometimes the rough – with his personality. The public loved him and followed him throughout his rounds. He used to spend ages before and after playing signing autographs and giving everybody of his time. Nothing was too much trouble for him. There have been few more popular sportsmen in the history of British sport.

KENNY LYNCH:

I followed Henry's career closely and it seems like only the day before yesterday that I saw him robbed against Joe Bugner.

It will soon be the fiftieth anniversary of when he floored Cassius Clay with his 'Ammer, the most famous punch ever thrown in a British ring. Those of us lucky enough to get close to him will remember him not so much as a great champion but as a wonderful human being, always looking to help those in need.

PETER ALLISS:

I have had three special Henrys in my life: Longhurst, the master of golf commentators; Cotton, arguably the greatest of all British golfers; and, of course, Cooper, a giant among men.

I think if Henry had been able to select he would have rather won the Open Golf Championship than the world heavyweight title. He loved the game, but was not blessed with the same natural ability that he showed in the boxing ring. Henry was always the first to offer his services when I was organising my charity golf tournaments. He was such a giving man, never taking.

Severiano Ballesteros departed in the same week as dear Henry. Losing two great men so close together is simply too much to bear.

KEITH SIMMONS, KING RAT OF THE ESTEEMED CHARITY FUNDRAISING SHOWBUSINESS FRATERNITY, THE GRAND ORDER OF WATER RATS:

Henry was a former King Rat, a charming companion who was always prepared to give his time to young and old, especially on behalf of the many charities he supported. A particularly generous action, which was typical, was when he was offered £10,000 to make an after-dinner speech. He discovered that the date clashed with an unpaid appearance at a Boy's Club, to which he had given his word that he would attend. He unhesitatingly refused the fat cheque.

Henry was a good boxer, but an outstanding man. A true Rat. The worlds of sport and showbusiness greatly mourn his passing, but his name and his deeds will always live on.

PAT JENNINGS, FORMER TOTTENHAM AND ARSENAL GOALKEEPER:

Henry and I used to compare our hand sizes, and he said he wished he'd had my size fists! When he was a boy he dreamt of becoming a goalkeeper like his old idol Frank Swift, but football's loss was boxing's gain.

He jokingly said that he only accepted me as a friend when I moved from Tottenham to play in goal for Arsenal. He was such a kindly, modest man, who made everybody he met feel special. I was so pleased to be at his Thanksgiving Service because I wanted to say farewell and pay my final respects to a great person.

KEN FRIAR, FOR MANY YEARS 'MR ARSENAL' AS THE CLUB'S MANAGING DIRECTOR:

We were very proud to have Henry as a VIP supporter of Arsenal. He represented the same sort of values as the club, competing with style and good sportsmanship. I was involved in all the organisational work when he challenged Muhammad Ali for the world heavyweight title at Highbury in 1966. What a night that was, and Henry was so unlucky that his old cut-eye curse struck.

He was a gentleman in and out of the ring. When he had his knee problems he used to come to the club to use our medical and training facilities. He was a joy to be around, always very friendly and without an ounce of arrogance. A true legend.

BOB WILSON, FORMER ARSENAL GOALKEEPER:

When Henry was recovering from his cartilage operation I was out of action with a broken arm, and the pair of us used to train together as we worked at getting our fitness back. He was a natural athlete and we formed an instant friendship. He was the most popular sportsman in the country, but did not have a boastful or conceited bone in his body. I can reveal that while he had a mighty left hook, he also had a hard right foot shot; I collected the ball from the back of the net many times during our kickabouts.

I learned two things from Henry – one, how to give 100 per cent at all times, whether inside sport or out; and two, the value of humility and tolerance.

Henry was a very special person and I was so pleased our paths crossed. My wife Megs and I will so miss not receiving the Cooper Christmas card, which was always the first to fall on our mat and it used to give us a tingle thinking how it had come from such a loving, family-oriented couple.

KEVIN KEEGAN:

Some of the most memorable and enjoyable times of my life were shooting the Brut commercials with Henry. As a young footballer I was a little bit nervous about meeting a national treasure, but he immediately put me at my ease and I loved every second of being in his company. He had loads of stories about the boxing game, but never told them in a showing-off way.

What always amazed me was how this kind, gentle, easygoing man ever got himself in the mood to punch people. Every time we met, long after the commercials, I used to say to him, 'Splash it all over,' and he'd reply, 'Ahhh, the sweet smell of Brut.' He was a lovely, lovely man and a great ambassador for his sport and for our country. If anybody deserved a knighthood, it was Our Enery.

LAWRIE McMENEMY:

I doubt if there has been another British sportsman who has reached into all hearts like Henry, regardless of whether they knew a left hook from a right cross. He became bigger than his sport and touched the lives of so many people, who were captured by his easygoing way and natural, unassuming nature. He was a Cockney, but people all over the country had an affinity with him, and he was as idolised in the North East, where I come from as in London.

Henry was always giving his time to help raise money and awareness for those less fortunate than he was, and his life was a shining example to today's young sportsmen, who could learn from his behaviour both when active in his sport and when he retired.

JOE BUGNER:

I'm so pleased Henry and I made our peace just a few years ago. It would have been so sad if he had gone to his resting place with us still divided by a controversial verdict. I was able to tell him how much I respected him, both as a boxer and even more so as a man. A hundred years from now, nobody will remember Joe Bugner, Frank Bruno, Lennox Lewis or David Haye – we will just be footnotes in history. But Henry Cooper will still be revered because his name will live on as a people's champion. Everybody in Britain loved him and there will never be another who can get close to his popularity. He proved by how long he reigned as British champion that he was a great boxer, and we all know he was a great person.

BILLY WALKER:

The trouble when I fought Henry was trying to get in the mood to dislike him enough to want to bash him. But he was a thorough gentleman and sporting at all times, even when he was making a mess of my face with that powerful left hand of his. He was well on top against me when the ref stopped it because of my cut eye. For a change it was not Henry who had been cut, and he was genuinely sympathetic and concerned for me. I can now admit I was lucky to get the cut because if the fight had gone on, he would have just about murdered me with that jab of his, and that's not counting his left hook!

We became mates after we'd finished hitting each other, and he was always a model for how boxers should conduct themselves both in and out of the ring. I felt honoured to be at his funeral, saying goodbye to a lovely bloke, whose name will always live on in British boxing.

FRANK BRUNO:

When I first turned professional, my manager Terry Lawless always told me I should copy Henry Cooper, not so much as a boxer but in the way he carried himself outside the ring. He was a class act, always finding time to help charities. I met him many times and found him to be a proper English gentleman. Don't think he rated me all that highly as a fighter, but he was entitled to his opinion.

We often worked together trying to raise money for the Water Rats, the Prince's Trust and Great Ormond Street Hospital. The man in the street loved him, and this was years after he had given up fighting. To remain that popular for so long shows just what a wonderful man he was outside the ring, and the fact that he gave Muhammad Ali so much trouble and was British champion for so many years proved he could really do the business inside the ring. He was a very special man. I felt honoured whenever I was in his company.

LENNOX LEWIS:

I found him a very amiable and modest man, and a wonderful representative for our sport. He was a legend in Britain and known around the world for that knockdown of Cassius Clay. The surprising thing about him – showing how boxing has changed – is that during his career he rarely weighed more than thirteen and a half stone but obviously he punched like a mule with his left hook.

BARRY McGUIGAN:

It was fitting to have Henry's wake at the London Golf Club because that's where he spent so much of his time. We were both members, and my wife and I became very friendly with Henry and the lovely Albina. He never recovered from her passing.

I first met him in London when I came over from Ireland to receive the Young Boxer of the Year award from the Boxing Writers' Club in the early 1980s. He went out of his way to talk to me and encourage me, and kindly followed my career from then on. Having Henry Cooper look out for me made me feel special. He was Mr Boxing.

The last time I saw him was at Harry Carpenter's memorial in Fleet Street, and he looked so frail that I was concerned for him. I prefer to think of him in the good times when he was warm, generous and with a great sense of humour. My feelings and sympathy are for Henry Marco and John Pietro, who have lost their dad and mum in a short space of time. They had parents who were always giving their time and energy for others, and they can be extremely proud of them. As somebody who loves boxing, let me just say that our sport has not had a better ambassador than Henry Cooper, Sir Henry, Our Enery.

DAVID HAYE:

Henry had retired long before I was born, but his exploits meant he was a legend and anybody who followed boxing knew all about him and the famous punch that knocked down the then Cassius Clay. It was a privilege for me to meet him, and I listened carefully to his advice, which he gave freely. He told me to pace my career, not rush things, and always to put fitness above everything. Coming from a true warrior and a great human being I listened with respect. There will never be another Henry Cooper.

AMIR KHAN:

I met Sir Henry several times, and he came across as very humble and willingly gave me advice on my career. He told me not to rush things, pick the right fights at the right time. He had a huge fan base, and every time I saw him he would spend ages signing autographs, never saying no to anybody. I love watching the film of him knocking down Muhammad Ali – or Cassius Clay as he was then – with a left hook that was beautifully delivered. If the bell had not gone, it was almost certain that he would have knocked him out because he was a great finisher. The man is a legend.

CHRIS EUBANK:

I was inspired by the beacon that was Henry Cooper. He was loved by the public and it inspired me to try to follow his example, but we are pretenders who can only walk in his shadow. He always behaved like a champion in and out of the ring, and is the perfect role model not only for boxers but also for any young sportsmen who need an example of how to behave. It was an honour to meet the great man, and when I shook his hand I just hoped the magic of Henry Cooper would rub off on me. He knew how to win the hearts of people. That is a gift given only to the finest human beings. Sir Henry had the gift in abundance.

STEVE COLLINS:

Just the name Henry Cooper was an inspiration to all boxers when I was first starting out in the game. We grew up with the stories of how he knocked Cassius Clay on his bum, and Enery's 'Ammer was part of boxing folklore. He had not been in the ring for forty years, but there was nobody in the fight game – and few outside it – who had not heard of him and his exploits. The way he gave so much of his time to good causes is an example to all sportsmen. He will never be forgotten.

FRANK WARREN:

Henry epitomised true British grit. He was one of sport's really nice guys, and the public identified with him because he always gave 100 per cent. He had not fought for forty years but remained the best loved of British sportsmen, even by generations who never saw him fight. He was unlucky that his chance of becoming world champion came against the greatest champion of all time, and he acquitted himself well before, as so often happened, he was cut.

Henry showed he had good taste by being an Arsenal fan. In these days of monster heavyweights, he would have had to fight in the cruiserweight division. People forget that early in his career he had four defeats on the trot, and he had to go abroad to reinstate himself. But what character he showed by fighting his way back to the top, and he won his way into the hearts of millions of people by his conduct and wonderfully natural personality. You could not manufacture what he had. Henry was a one-off.

BARRY HEARN:

Our best-loved boxer will be remembered for all time because of throwing the most famous punch in British boxing history, the left hook that put Cassius Clay down. Domestically he was the master heavyweight, as is proven by his reign of nearly twelve years as British champion.

These days of course he would be considered a cruiserweight because he never weighed even fourteen stone, but that 'Ammer of his could take out anybody. Most times I met him over the last twenty or thirty years he was giving his time to fundraising for the disadvantaged, and he seemed to live on the golf course, where he was always playing in charity events. He put back much more than he took out.

BERNARD HART, FORMER WELTERWEIGHT WHO FOUNDED THE FAMOUS LONSDALE SPORTS GOODS COMPANY:

The twins and I used to box as amateurs for the Eltham club, and in those days George was considered just as bright a prospect as Henry. Then he started having trouble with his right hand, which was every bit as lethal as Henry's left. They were lovely blokes, always good for a laugh but taking their boxing very seriously. Whenever they were on the bill, crowds flocked to see them at Eltham Baths, back in the days when amateur boxing was really flourishing.

There's talk about building a statue to Henry on the Bellingham council estate where he grew up. I'd give my support to that. I cannot think of a better role model for the kids on that estate or anywhere else. Henry was a credit to the area, a credit to boxing and a credit to the country.

TERRY BAKER, AN ENTREPRENEUR WHO, WITH HIS WIFE FREDA, RUNS THE A1 SPORTING SPEAKERS AGENCY THAT SET UP MANY ROAD SHOW APPEARANCES FOR HENRY:

I booked Henry for a few evenings for theatre shows and we hit it off immediately. Obviously not a hard thing to do with Henry because just about everyone that ever met him felt the same way. He epitomised the saying, 'What you see is what you get'. He really was the nicest man you could wish to meet. How he ever hit anybody is hard to imagine!

Every time we worked with him, Freda and I would receive a bouquet with a card saying, 'Thanks for a great evening, all the best, love from Henry'. Eventually I said to him, 'I'm glad you enjoy working with us, Henry, and I appreciate the gesture, but I never thought in my wildest dreams that at some stage in my life I would regularly receive flowers from a heavyweight boxer!'

'Oh,' he replied, 'that will be Albina. She must be sending them as

One of the last action shots of Our Enery as he goes toe to toe with Joe Bugner in his final fight at Wembley Arena in 1971. The fifteen rounds points decision and the three titles went to 21-year-old Bugner. The public sympathy went to 37-year-old Henry.

Henry the doting dad, playing with his sons John Pietro (left) and Henry Marco the year after he hung up his gloves to follow a career as a full-time celebrity and charity fund-raiser. Oh yes, and as a golfer.

Sir Henry with the love of his life, Lady Albina Cooper, loved and admired by everybody who came into contact with her. She was Henry's strength and shield and he never recovered from her passing in 2008.

Henry's most treasured possessions were his hard-earned Lonsdale Belts. No other boxer in history has ever won three of them outright. That is an empty smile above, as he prepares to put his Belts up for auction after his savings had been wiped out by the crash of the Lloyd's Names syndicate. He was advised he could get as much as £100,000 for the Belts, which eventually went under the hammer (not Enery's 'Ammer) for a disappointing £42,000, but it was enough to save the Coopers from bankruptcy.

In happier times, Henry popularised a national catchphrase with 'Splash it all over' from his series of Brut television commercials, including in the company of football idol Kevin Keegan. They became firm friends.

Granddad Henry has just become Sir Henry, and helping him celebrate at Buckingham Palace is grandson Henry James.

Henry had earlier become a Papal knight, honoured from Rome for his charity work, and it was Cardinal Hume who conferred the knighthood on behalf of the Pope.

Never happier than when on the golf course, Henry clowns around with comedian pal Jimmy Tarbuck and his golfing hero Seve Ballesteros, who sadly passed on in 2011, in the same week as Our Enery.

Henry had not finished jabbing. He was the front man for a successful fight-the-flu television and poster campaign for senior citizens, inspiring pensioners with the challenge: 'Don't get knocked out by flu, get your jab in first.'

Comfortable in the presence of princes or paupers, Henry was a king in his own right when ruling over the great showbusiness charity, the Grand Order of Water Rats, as King Rat, with the Duke of Edinburgh among his subjects.

Later he became equally popular with the Duke's grandson Prince William when helping to raise funds for Sport Relief. Sir Henry generated millions of pounds for charity during his lifetime.

Henry was the first sportsman to win the coveted BBC Sports Personality of the Year award twice, before presenting it to his successor Princess Anne, popular with viewers for her Olympic equestrian performances. He met Prince Charles on scores of occasions, chiefly when helping to raise funds for the Prince's Trust. Henry was a particular favourite of the Queen Mother, and he had a portrait of her on the wall at his home in Kent.

Good friends after they finished hitting each other, Muhammad Ali and Henry are reunited in London in 1993 on the thirtieth anniversary of their famous Wembley fight.

The last journey for Henry. Hundreds of people lined the streets of Surrey to pay their final respects as the funeral car took the folk hero to a thanksgiving service in Tonbridge, Kent, before a private crematorium ceremony when Henry's ashes were mixed with those of his beloved Albina.

a thank you because she knows how much I appreciate all the jobs you get me and how you always come and make it easy for me.'

'Thank goodness for that,' I replied, 'I thought *you* were sending them!' Albina was as lovely as her husband, but I'm glad the flowers were from her and the gesture was always appreciated. Freda and I felt blessed to have known Henry. He was unique.

Henry's fame was worldwide. The week after he passed on there was a Bob Arum promotion in Las Vegas featuring Manny Pacquiao's world welterweight title defence against Shane Mosley and before the fight the capacity crowd paid their respects in silence during a ten-second tolling of the bell in Henry's memory.

BOB ARUM:

Henry epitomised what you want your champion boxer to be – dignified, sporting, dedicated, no trash-talking; but when he got in the ring, that's when you saw his heart and determination. Sadly for him, the one thing he could not toughen was his skin and he bled all too easily. But he was a great fighter and a great man, and for those of us lucky to have known him, he will be missed. He served boxing well, and will be remembered on both sides of the Atlantic with warmth and respect.

GEORGE FOREMAN:

Henry came so close to changing the history of boxing. Had he landed his left hook on Clay's jaw in the early part of the fourth round instead of the final seconds, he would have wrecked a lot of big plans. The fight with Sonny Liston would not have taken place when it did. It would have been a whole different picture. Maybe I would not have got beaten up in Zaire! Henry's spirit was always willing, but unfortunately for him the flesh was often weak.

He was a real English gentleman and very popular on both sides of the pond. Henry was one of the greatest heavyweight fighters never to win the world title, a boxer and a man of real class.

ANGELO DUNDEE:

Without doubt, Henry was one of the nicest guys I ever met in the
boxing business. He had every reason to be bitter towards me because
of the chicanery I got up to with the torn glove in that first fight with
Cassius, but he accepted it as part and parcel of a tough profession.
I'd just like to go on record and say I didn't use scissors to worsen the
tear, just a little thumb work. If I'd been in Henry's corner he would
have expected me to do the same thing, buying precious time.

My brother Chris and I got to know Henry and his great character
of a manager, Jim Wicks, really well and you could not wish to meet
more likeable people. The left hook with which he hit Cassius – later
Muhammad Ali, of course – was the hardest my guy had ever been
hit. When he wobbled back to the corner, we used more ice to revive
him than sank the *Titanic*.

Henry and I were last together when he came over to the States to be inducted into our Boxing Hall of Fame. Only the greatest fighters get that honour. Henry Cooper was a great fighter, and a fine man who inspired several generations of British boxers.

Both Henry and I recently lost our wives, and it's hard to handle. Henry struggled but now, please God, he is reunited with his beloved Albina. We were in opposite corners in the boxing ring, but in the same corner in life. I have lost a true friend.

CLIFF MORGAN, WELSH RUGBY LEGEND AND HENRY'S RIVAL TEAM CAPTAIN ON *A QUESTION OF SPORT*:

Oh, what a magical times they were. Henry was an absolute joy to work with, always in such a good mood and with warm smiles and barrel-loads of bonhomie that he poured on everybody in the studio. He was never self-conscious about breaking grammatical rules, and I think that was a big part of his appeal. He was a complete natural, and never tried to be something that he wasn't. His all-round knowledge of sport was about average when he first started the show, but before the first series was even halfway, though he had done his homework so thoroughly that he was like a walking record book, and that attention to detail captured the way he approached any task.

I was privileged to be at his Thanksgiving Service, which I would not have missed for the world. These days I am something of a crumbling building, but I made it there on my sticks. Nothing would have stopped me. I wanted to say my final farewell to a good friend and a great humanitarian.

DES LYNAM:

It was Cliff Morgan, when head of the BBC radio sports department, who paired Henry and me as his radio boxing commentary team. That stroke of luck gave me many happy years in the company of the great man as we covered numerous world, European and British title fights.

Henry's job was to fill the minute between rounds with his comments. He often found remembering people's names quite difficult. Our producer for many of the years together was called Phil. Henry never called him anything but John, a bit like Trigger and 'Dave' in *Only Fools and Horses*. I once rang him to check he was available for a forthcoming fight. 'I've already had a call from your colleague Ben Burgess,' he said. The man's name was Bob Burrows.

When Alan Minter lost his 1980 world middleweight title fight against Marvin Hagler and some of his fans started hurling bottles at the ring, Henry was the first to duck under the ring apron to avoid injury. I teased him about it afterwards. 'You disappeared a bit quick,' I said. 'I didn't mind getting cut when I was getting paid for it,' he explained, 'but I wasn't risking it for nothing.'

JOHN RAWLING:

I followed Des Lynam and Ian Darke as BBC radio commentator and inherited Henry as my co-commentator. His iconic status meant that he was mobbed by autograph hunters wherever we were, to the extent that I would frequently feel more like a minder than a colleague. 'Come on, Henry, we've got to get out of here to record that interview,' was the stock excuse that I would give to let him eventually walk away and make his exit from the arena. He would go to any lengths necessary to help a charity, even if it meant giving up a well-paid engagement. Henry was a good boxer, an outstanding man.

IAN DARKE:

I worked on BBC radio with Henry as the inter-rounds summariser for about eight years. A little anecdote that sums up his influence was when we were commentating on a Tony Sibson fight at Stafford. All hell broke loose in the hall and the crowd were rioting and throwing things like CS canisters. In desperation, the MC came to us at the ringside and asked, 'Henry, can you do something about this, please?' Without further ado, he clambered up into the ring and said into the MC's microphone, 'For goodness' sake, everybody calm down, will you, and sit down so we can get on with the boxing.' There were all kinds of ruffians and troublemakers just looking for a fight, but once they realised who was ordering them back to their seats they went and sat down like little lambs. It was then I fully appreciated the power that Henry had and the reverence and respect he commanded.

He had a great sense of humour. Once we were doing a broadcast on April Fool's Day, and between us we cooked up the idea of him announcing that he was training for a comeback and was going to fight Brian London. It was supposed to tease the public, but Fleet Street picked up on it and believed it, and we were suddenly inundated with calls about the details of Henry's return to the ring.

We had to bashfully admit it was an April Fool's Day joke. Henry could not stop chuckling over it. He was about fifty-eight, for goodness' sake.

HUGH McILVANNEY OF THE *SUNDAY TIMES*, ARGUABLY THE GREATEST SPORTS WRITER OF MY GENERATION:

For Henry, modesty wasn't a chosen public demeanour. It was as natural to him as smiling, which he did often and with an unmistakable warm-heartedness that reached out like an embrace to everybody around him, and ultimately to an entire nation. His truest distinction was bestowed by the masses, who granted him a popularity unsurpassed for intensity and longevity in the history of sport in this country. Henry was worthy of it all.

My many memories of him glow with the awareness that every moment spent in his company left me feeling better for it. He had the knack of being a good human being. People who had never attended a fight, who didn't have an inkling that his reign of nearly twelve years as British heavyweight champion was a record never likely to be broken, felt they had a personal, almost proprietorial stake in Our Enery.

COLIN HART, BOXING COLUMNIST AT *THE SUN*:

If Henry had been made out of bricks and mortar he would have been a Grade I listed building, because unquestionably he was a national treasure. He was my mate for more years than I care to remember and his loss will be felt in every British home.

Describing Henry as a fighter and a man isn't difficult as he can be summed up in a few words. They are integrity, goodness and honesty. He was always a genuine role model for young and old. If the paparazzi had to rely on him for a living they would have starved. Not for him getting drunk in nightclubs surrounded by bimbos. His priorities were always his family and working hard raising money for various charities.

I knew he was in trouble the moment Albina went so suddenly, and then followed soon after by George. Albina was not just his right hand but also his left, and his eyes and ears. I have rarely known such a close couple, and for the first time in his life he threw in the towel. Dear Henry has left a unique legacy and British boxing is a far sadder place for his passing.

That's the Henry Cooper life. Now for his fights.

THE HENRY COOPER FIGHT FILE

enry and I used to have a chuckle because I remembered his fights blow-for-blow much better than he did. 'Yeah,' he would say, 'but you had the easy part of watching while I was a little busy doing the fighting.'

As a boxing-mad schoolboy and later as a reporter on the fight trade paper *Boxing News*, I used to fervently keep records of all the major fighters. So this section is something of a labour of love, and – excuse the bugle-blowing – gives the most exhaustive breakdown of our hero's professional boxing career you are likely to find anywhere. It was made easier by the fact that Henry and I spent hours discussing his career for a book we worked on together, *Henry Cooper's Most Memorable Fights*. Our interview sessions included access to his personal scrapbook, dripping with punchlines from the finest British boxing writers of that golden era for heavyweights and for Fleet Street.

Those were the days when every newspaper carried at least one specialist boxing reporter, the headline-hungry epoch of masters of the art such as Peter 'The Man They Can't Gag' Wilson, Desmond

'The Man in the Brown Bowler' Hackett, Tom 'Who Will He Put His Shirt On?' Phillips, 'Frank and Fearless' Frank Butler, the redoubtable Donald Saunders on the *Telegraph*, the omniscient freelance Gilbert Odd, reliable Joe Bromley on *The Sporting Life*, Henry's Wembley neighbour on the London *Evening Star*, Walter Bartleman, the

'Terrible Twins' Reg Gutteridge and Harry Carpenter before they ever picked up a microphone, and the most sublime of them all, George Whiting, who could single-handedly put thousands on the London *Evening Standard* circulation by his poetic presence at the ringside. On the *Daily Express* they had the luxury of two ringside experts, with Sydney Hulls, son of the premier pre-war promoter of the same name, playing a supporting role to the adjective-addicted Des Hackett.

Boxing News was the Bible of the sport, and from America we drank in the international facts from *The Ring* magazine and *Boxing Illustrated*. Learning the writing ropes as Henry started out on his boxing adventure were young Turks like Neil Allen at *The Times*, Alan Hubbard, Peter Moss, Frank McGhee, John Rodda, Ron Wills, Bill Bateson, Fred Burcombe, Frank Keating, Bob Mee, Jeff Powell, Kevin Mitchell, Steve Bunce, Peter Batt, Hugh McIlvanney and – now the doyen of boxing scribes – Colin Hart, for whom the *Sun* still rises.

I bow to them all as exceptional reporters back in the day when newspapers treated boxing and boxers with the respect they deserved, rather than giving the sport second billing. Henry was a hero to each of them, and he knew all of them personally, but could rarely put a name to their faces.

People meeting Henry in his later life and hearing him struggle to remember names put it down to the punches he had taken, not realising that for the fifty-plus years that I had known him he could seldom get anybody's name off his tongue at the first time of asking. Johns became Joes, Bills Bobs and Timmys Tommys. Talking to me once about his broadcasting colleague and good pal Des Lynam, he referred to him as 'Les Dynam'. Those of us who knew him well were amazed how he managed to come up with so many correct names when he was the resident captain on *A Question of Sport*. Mind you, he did once manage to call Don Bradman 'Brad Donman'. Jim Wicks was full of malapropisms and Henry a master Spoonerist – the perfect double act.

I recall Henry, George and me going into convulsions of laughter in my early days of being in their company when Jim Wicks was, as ever, struggling to get a name right. He was talking in less than favourable terms of the Chancellor of the Exchequer at the time, Selwyn Lloyd. 'That robbing bastard of a Chancellor geezer, wossisname…' he said. Together, literally identically, the twins chorused: 'Selwyn Thingamybob…'

A Jim Wicks press conference was always a 'fill in the blanks' affair. He would continually refer to upcoming or past opponents as 'wossisname' and somehow this became contagious because Henry and George could never come up with a surname between them. Henry always introduced me to people as 'Norman, uh…' and his co-commentators in his many boxing broadcasts used to tell him to leave the name-calling to them because he invariably got boxers' names wrong. Once, on air, he hilariously called the then heavyweight title challenger Herbie Hide 'Harry Herbert'.

I can guarantee that all the names in the following fight file are correct, and I thank the various newspaper editors for their permission to use the scrapbook reports from a procession of Britain's finest boxing reporters.

For the record, Henry the amateur had eighty-four contests, won seventy-three and lost eleven. He collected two back-to-back ABA light-heavyweight titles, the first in 1952 while boxing for the Eltham and District Amateur Boxing Club, and the second in 1953, while serving in the Army. He represented Britain in the 1952 Olympics in Helsinki and in the 1953 European championships in Warsaw, each time going out in the early stages to older and much more experienced Russian opponents: Anatoli Perov (lost a split points decision) and then Juri Jegorow (referee stopped contest 1). His finest performance was his 1953 ABA final points win over Australian Tony Madigan, recognised as one of the supreme amateur boxers of his generation, who gave Cassius Clay his hardest contest in the 1960 Olympics.

Henry made his professional debut on a Jack Solomons promotion at Harringay Arena in North London, a huge, soulless, grey concrete octagonal stadium that was the number one boxing venue until 1958. It was built in the 1930s as a home for the brief British craze for ice hockey and was virtually a copy of the famous Maple Leaf Gardens in Toronto. Henry and twin brother George (billed as Jim Cooper) were featured in the second and third fights before the top-of-the-bill British middleweight championship contest in which Johnny Sullivan knocked out Gordon Hazell in the first round.

FIGHT NO. 1

- Venue: Harringay Arena, 14 September 1954. Weight: 13st 7lb.
- Opponent: HARRY PAINTER (Andover, Hants). Weight: 14st 13lb.
- Result: WON by knockout, round 1.

RINGSIDE REPORT (JT Hulls, London *Evening News*): Bellingham heavyweight Henry Cooper made an impressive professional debut against workhorse veteran Harry Painter, who has shown little improvement since winning the Jack Solomons's Novices competition. Plasterer Cooper decorated Painter's face with a series of left jabs before dropping him with a hook off the jab. Painter unwisely and unsteadily rose at 'eight' and was an easy target for Cooper's favourite left hook that knocked him down and out, with the ten-second count a mere formality. It won't get easier than this for the two-time ABA light-heavyweight champion. Twin brother

George had a much harder night's work, winning a six rounds' slog on points against Newport bulldozer Dick Richardson. I am proud to have introduced the Cooper twins to manager Jim Wicks. They are perfectly suited and I expect them to be very successful in the demanding world of professional boxing.

HENRY: I'm glad to have got that over. I was concerned about giving away so much weight, but Mr Wicks told me to take my time and pick my punches. I found Harry easy to hit with my jab, and I concentrated on making an opening for my left hook. Mr Wicks is happy, so I'm happy.

FIGHT NO. 2

- Venue: Harringay Arena, 19 October 1954. Weight: 13st 8lb.
- Opponent: DINNY POWELL (Walworth). Weight: 13st 12lb.
- Result: WON, referee stopped fight round 4.

RINGSIDE REPORT (L.N. Bailey, London *Evening Star*): A handful of miles separate where Henry Cooper and Dinny Powell grew up in South-East London, but there was a huge distance between them in class. Cooper, in his second professional fight, jabbed the stocky Powell almost to a standstill, and you felt Dinny needed his brother Nosher Powell in the ring with him to block the procession of left jabs that made a mess of his face and forced the referee's intervention in round four of a scheduled six-rounder. Even at this early stage in his career, Cooper looks a class act.

HENRY: To be honest, the only trouble Dinny gave me was with his head as he came rushing forward. This sort of thing didn't happen in the amateurs and it was good experience to see how I could handle being roughed up inside by an experienced pro. I know the Powell brothers well, and they're making names for themselves in the film stuntman business. They're good blokes, but you forget friendship once the bell rings.

FIGHT NO. 3

- Venue: Manor Place Baths, Walworth, 23 November 1954. Weight: 13st 6lb.
- Opponent: Eddie Keith (Manchester). Weight: 13st 4lb.
- Result: WON, referee stopped fight round 1.

RINGSIDE REPORT (George Whiting, London *Evening Standard*): Henry Cooper, the more lethal of the Cooper twins, wasted no time parting Eddie Keith from his senses, and the referee came to his rescue after a barrage of left hooks midway through the first round had him distressed and disoriented. Keep your eye on young Henry. The professional game seems to suit him very nicely.

HENRY: The ref was right to step in when he did because Ted was struggling in there once I had softened him up with a couple of good hooks. It would be nice if all fights were this easy, but Mr Wicks is slowly going to step me up in class.

FIGHT NO. 4

- Venue: Harringay Arena, 7 December 1954. Weight: 13st 4lb.
- Opponent: Denny Ball (Bedford). Weight: 14st 7lb.
- Result: WON, referee stopped fight round 3.

RINGSIDE REPORT (Dave Caldwell, *South London Press*): Henry Cooper gave away more than a stone to his opponent Denny Ball, but was a much more potent puncher and the burly man from Bedford folded under a series of lefts to the head. The referee quite rightly stepped in to save Ball more punishment in the third round.

HENRY: As Denny had gone the distance against my old rival Joe Erskine earlier this year, I expected him to put up more resistance. But once I found my range I was confident I'd stop him, and I think he was relieved when the ref said that was enough.

FIGHT NO. 5

- Venue: Royal Albert Hall, 27 January 1955. Weight: 13st 5lb.
- Opponent: Colin Strauch (Pretoria). Weight: 13st 2lb.
- Result: WON, referee stopped fight round 1.

RINGSIDE REPORT (Joe Bromley, *Sporting Life*): Colin Strauch has come over from South Africa to try to make a name for himself. Well, last night at the Albert Hall he did not know what his name was after Henry Cooper landed a peach of a left hook that had him rolling and reeling before the referee came to his rescue barely two minutes into the first round. Henry Cooper is a heavyweight who is going to make a huge impact with that left hook of his. It is a mighty weapon.

HENRY: We thought we might get a few rounds under our belt tonight, but Strauch did not give us as much trouble as we expected. It was a nice way to start the New Year, particularly at one of our favourite venues. There's a special atmosphere here at the Albert Hall.

FIGHT NO. 6

- Venue: Harringay Arena, 8 February 1955. Weight: 13st 9lb.
- Opponent: Cliff Purnell (Weston-super-Mare). Weight: 13st 11lb.
- Result: WON points, 6 rounds.

RINGSIDE REPORT (Harry Carpenter, *Daily Mail*): Manager Jim Wicks did not mince words after his brightest prospect, Henry Cooper, was taken the distance for the first time since he turned professional. 'Southpaws,' he said, 'should be drowned at birth. He made our Enery look bad, in fact he would make Marilyn Monroe look bad.' Cooper was a comfortable points winner over six untidy rounds, but struggled to find his rhythm and timing against an experienced opponent who knows all the tricks of the trade and made the Bellingham plasterer work hard for his win.

HENRY: The only good thing to say about tonight is that at least we know we can go six rounds comfortably. Purnell was an awkward cuss, and when I pinned him with a good punch he'd pull me in close and hold on. I learned some useful pro tricks from him. I only fought a handful of southpaws as an amateur and never enjoyed it. And to think I'd have been a wrong-way-round merchant if my first trainer had not rollocked me for leading with my right.

FIGHT NO. 7

- Venue: Earls Court, 8 March 1955. Weight: 13st 7lb.
- Opponent: Hugh Ferns (Greenock). Weight: 15st 4lb.
- Result: WON on a disqualification, round 2.

RINGSIDE REPORT (Sydney Hulls, *Daily Express*): Hugh Ferns, former Scottish amateur heavyweight champion, came rushing at Henry Cooper like a wild Angus bull, and the referee had no option but to disqualify him in the second round after he had butted the Bellingham plasterer and landed with blows way off the compass. It is all part of the learning curve for Cooper, who is definitely one to watch for the future.

HENRY: Ferns was using his head like a third glove, and his punches were landing well south of the border. A win like this leaves you feeling frustrated. He was a big target and we'd just about got his measure when the ref threw him out.

FIGHT NO. 8

- Venue: Empress Hall, Earls Court, 19 March 1955. Weight: 13st 7lb.
- Opponent: Joe Crickmar (Stepney). Weight: 13st 2lb.
- Result: WON, referee stopped fight round 5.

RINGSIDE REPORT (Jack Wilson, *Boxing News*): Bellingham's undefeated Henry Cooper chalked up his eighth successive victory with a commanding performance against Joe Crickmar, the pride of the Arbour Youth Club in Stepney. Cooper completely dominated the fight with his powerful left jab and thunderous hooks, and the referee stopped the one-way traffic with Crickmar suffering severe facial damage.

HENRY: We're pleased with that performance because Joe's a good boxer, but he never really troubled us. As soon as I got the old trombone left working he couldn't get out of the way of it, and I knew it was just a question of time before the referee would have to step in. Poor old Joe cuts worse than we do.

FIGHT NO. 9

- Venue: Manor Place Baths, Walworth, 19 March 1955. Weight: 13st 7lb.
- Opponent: Joe Bygraves (Jamaica/Birkenhead). Weight: 14st 5lb.
- Result: WON points, 8 rounds.

RINGSIDE REPORT (Walter Bartleman, London *Evening Star*): Henry Cooper produced the best performance of his career to date with a clear points victory over Merseyside-based Joe Bygraves. It was Cooper's first eight rounds contest, and proof that he travelled the distance comfortably is that he dropped Bygraves for an eight count in the final round and only the bell saved the heavily muscled Jamaican from a stoppage defeat.

HENRY: We paced it nicely, and we felt so strong in the last round we went for a knockout. Joe was wobbling at the end and if there had been a few more seconds I think we'd have finished him off. We're chuffed with that performance, easily our best so far.

'Henry on the attack in his first fight with Jamaican Joe Bygraves in 1955'

FIGHT NO. 10

- Venue: Harringay Arena, 26 April 1955. Weight: 13st 4lb.
- Opponent: Uber Bacilieri (Italy). Weight: 14st 2lb.
- Result: LOST, referee stopped fight round 2 (cut eye).

RINGSIDE REPORT (Bill McGowran, London *Evening News*): Henry Cooper's unbeaten record came to a gruesome end against Italian champion Uber Bacilieri, drowned in a river of blood that flowed from a nasty cut on his brow. The injury seemed to be caused by a clash of heads, although the Italian's camp claimed it was from a punch. Cooper was just beginning to take control with his thumping left lead at the time of the abrupt finish.

HENRY: Jim had already decided to stop the fight as the referee waved it over. We didn't want to risk the cut getting any worse. It was definitely his head that caused the damage, but what's the point in complaining? I just want to get back into the ring again as soon as possible. I've got so much unused energy to burn.

FIGHT NO. 11

- Venue: Nottingham Ice Rink, 6 June 1955. Weight: 13st 4lb.
- Opponent: Ron Harman (Brighton). Weight: 14st 7lb.
- Result: WON, referee stopped fight round 7.

RINGSIDE REPORT (Peter Wilson, *Daily Mirror*): The last time I saw Brighton heavyweight Ron Harman was when he fought on the undercard on the Rocky Marciano/Don Cockell world title promotion in San Francisco, and he dispatched an American opponent in style. Here at Nottingham it was his turn to be dispatched, with equal violence, by Henry Cooper, a stylish young fighter whom his manager Jim Wicks tells me is 'going to go all the way'. He certainly has impressive power in that left hand of his, and Harman needed to be rescued by the referee in the seventh round after taking quite a tanking.

HENRY: Ron really knows the ropes and we had to be at our best to beat him. It was good to get some rounds under our belt, and now we're going to try to put the record straight by getting a rematch with that Italian geezer who stopped our unbeaten run.

FIGHT NO. 12

- Venue: White City Stadium, 13 September 1955. Weight: 13st 1lb.
- Opponent: Uber Bacilieri (Italy). Weight: 14st.
- Result: WON, knockout round 7.

RINGSIDE REPORT (Joe Bromley, *Sporting Life*): Henry Cooper gained sweet and savage revenge for his only defeat when he knocked out Uber Bacilieri in seven one-sided rounds. The Italian had beaten Cooper on a cut-eye stoppage five months ago, but was made to pay for it in an agonising way. Cooper peppered his face with a procession of solid left jabs before suddenly switching the attack to the body. A left-right combination deep into the pit of the stomach left Bacilieri writhing in pain on the canvas as the referee counted him out.

HENRY: This was an important victory for us because we proved that defeat by Bacilieri was misleading. Jim told me to go for the body at the end of the sixth, and it worked to perfection. He had been eating my jab and was getting his guard higher and higher to try to block it, leaving his body as a very inviting target.

FIGHT NO. 13

- Venue: Harringay Arena, 15 November 1955. Weight: 13st 2lb.
- Opponent: Joe Erskine (Cardiff). Weight: 14st 1lb.
- Result: LOST points, 10 rounds (British title eliminator)

RINGSIDE REPORT (George Whiting, London *Evening Standard*): Familiarity breeds contempt, and Joe Erskine was quite contemptuous of his old amateur rival Henry Cooper, winning this British heavyweight title eliminator with a cleverly compiled points victory. As hard as Cooper tried, he could not land that pay-off left hook because the will o' the wisp Welshman was never there to be hit.

HENRY: Not making excuses, but I badly bruised my hand on Joe's head in the seventh round, which reduced my power. No complaints. He deserved his victory, and we hope he now goes on and wins the British title. Joe boxed beautifully, and we are now two-two. One day we must meet again to sort out our private argument.

FIGHT NO. 14

- Venue: Royal Albert Hall, 2 February 1956. Weight: 13st 8lb.
- Opponent: Maurice Mols (France). Weight: 14st 4lb.
- Result: WON, referee stopped fight round 4.

RINGSIDE REPORT (Tom Phillips, *Daily Herald*): Henry Cooper got back to his winning ways with a chilling execution of roly-poly

Frenchman Maurice Mols, who looked like the Michelin Tyre Man but less mobile. It took three rounds for Cooper to find his distance against an opponent who hid behind a high guard, but when he found his range the overweight, overmatched Mols was quickly deflated. Referee Tommy Little rescued the forlorn Frenchman after he had made four visits to the canvas in round four.

HENRY: This was good for my confidence. We were surprised that Mols did not look that well prepared considering he's the French champion. I just got on and did my job, and those spare tyres round his tummy made a nice target.

FIGHT NO. 15

- Venue: Empress Hall, Earls Court, 1 May 1956. Weight: 13st 4lb.
- Opponent: Brian London (Blackpool). Weight: 13st 13lb.
- Result: WON, referee stopped fight round 1.

RINGSIDE REPORT (Peter Wilson, *Daily Mirror*): Brian London had no idea what hit him at the Empress Hall last night. Let me tell him – it was a perfect left hook from Henry Cooper that knocked the Blackpool heavyweight back into a neutral corner, literally out on his feet. The referee waved it all over after just two minutes twenty-five seconds of round one, without the previously unbeaten London having landed one telling blow. The Blackpool Rock was reduced to candyfloss. London was having his thirteenth fight and weighed in at 13st 13lb. Unlucky for some, certainly for the blitzed London!

HENRY: This is sweet revenge for what London did to my brother George when they fought in January. Brian did a lot of bad-mouthing before the fight, but I think I taught him to be more respectful. We like to let our fists do the talking.

'Brian London finds that Henry can also hurt with his right hand'

FIGHT NO. 16

- Venue: Empire Pool, Wembley, 26 June 1956. Weight: 13st 6lb.
- Opponent: Giannino Luise (Italy). Weight: 15st.
- Result: WON, referee stopped fight round 7.

RINGSIDE REPORT (Johnny Sharpe, *Ring Magazine*): Henry Cooper, tall, upright, stylish heavyweight in the tradition of English fighters of old, won every round against the lumbering Giannino Luise, pummelling him with a stream of left jabs to the head. In round seven he switched his attack to the body, and a left hook to the liver made the Italian whelp with pain and he sank backwards and fell under the bottom rope. He managed to scramble back into the ring with the count at nine, but the referee sensibly stopped the contest as the hard-punching Cooper moved in for the kill.

HENRY: To be honest, I'd never even heard of the guy and had nothing to go on about his style, so I was playing it by ear. He was a hard nut who soaked up punches that would have floored most opponents, but the punch to the liver finished him off and the referee did him a big favour by stopping it when he did.

FIGHT NO. 17

- Venue: King's Hall, Belle Vue, Manchester, 7 September 1956. Weight: 13st 4lb.
- Opponent: Peter Bates (Shirebrook, Derbyshire). Weight: 14st 11lb.
- Result: LOST, retired end of round 5 (cut eye).

RINGSIDE REPORT (Walter Bartleman, London *Evening Star*): The cut eye curse that is blighting the career of Jim Cooper now seems to have claimed his identical twin brother Henry. The Bellingham heavyweight was well on top against Peter Bates when he came out of a fifth round clinch with blood pouring from a cut, and at the bell manager Jim Wicks had no hesitation in retiring his fighter. I thought Cooper had won the fight in the first round when he floored Bates with a cracking left hook, and as he staggered up at nine he seemed in no position to defend himself, yet the referee allowed them to fight on. Bates was often shaken by Cooper's power throughout the fight and he must have been a relieved and surprised man to have his hand raised in victory.

HENRY: What a choker. I was looking for an opening to finish it when he caught me as we came together in a clinch. I knew straight away it was a bad cut, and as I walked back to the corner at the bell Jim was already calling the ref over. Just one of those things. We thought it wisest to call it a day at the end of the round rather than risk making it worse.

FIGHT NO. 18

- Venue: Earls Court, 19 February 1957. Weight: 13st 13lb.
- Opponent: Joe Bygraves (Jamaica/Birkenhead). Weight: 14st 6lb.
- Result: LOST, knocked out round 9 (British Empire heavyweight title).

RINGSIDE REPORT (Donald Saunders, *Daily Telegraph*): Usually the most elegant of boxers, Henry Cooper was reduced to a pitiful puppet of pain by a perfect punch to the solar plexus from Birkenhead-based Jamaican Joe Bygraves, who claimed the prize of the vacant Empire heavyweight championship. The dramatic finish to a rough and tumble fight came in the ninth round. Cooper had been dropped by a combination to the jaw, but seemed in control of himself when he got up at nine. Bygraves, a magnificently built man who appears to have muscles on his muscles, charged forward and threw a wicked punch to the body, and it literally took Cooper's breath away and he was gasping for air as he took the ten second count on his knees.

HENRY: That was the worst moment I've ever known in a boxing ring. I was really fighting for my breath and there was no way I could continue. I boxed badly and just could not get into my usual rhythm. Good luck to Joe. We used to be teammates with the England amateur squad, and he's a good fellah. I felt really sluggish tonight, and will never again come into the ring this heavy.

FIGHT NO. 19

- Venue: Johanneshov Ice Stadium, Stockholm, 19 May 1957. Weight: 13st 11lb.
- Opponent: Ingemar Johansson (Sweden). Weight: 14st 4lb.
- Result: LOST, knocked out round 5 (European heavyweight title).

RINGSIDE REPORT (Tom Phillips, *Daily Herald*): Ingemar Johansson threw one meaningful punch in defence of his European title and it was enough to drop Henry Cooper on to his knees for the ten second count. I was busier typing than they were fighting for the first four rounds that featured Johansson pawing rather than punching and Cooper retreating as if in anticipation of the Swede's famous Ingo's Bingo punch. It arrived eventually, crashing against Cooper's jaw as he squinted looking into a bright sun setting on a sprawling open-air arena. Suddenly the sun went out for Cooper as he crashed to a third successive defeat.

HENRY: I know this will sound corny but I honestly didn't see the punch coming. The sun was in my eyes, and then boom – I was on the deck. I should have stuck to our pre-fight plan to concentrate on counter punching, but I got frustrated and went after him. Not the wisest thing I've ever done.

FIGHT NO. 20

- Venue: Harringay Arena, 17 September 1957. Weight: 13st 6lb.
- Opponent: Joe Erskine (Cardiff). Weight: 14st 2lb.
- Result: LOST points 15 rounds (British heavyweight title).

RINGSIDE REPORT (Frank McGhee, *Daily Mirror*): Henry Cooper looked on open-mouthed in amazement like a man who'd had his pocket picked in an empty room as referee Eugene Henderson held up Joe Erskine's hand as the points winner at the end of this frankly tedious fifteen rounds British championship contest. I made Cooper a winner by a quarter of a point, but the biased London crowd, Cooper fans to a man, booed angrily when Welshman Erskine had the Lonsdale Belt hooked around his waist.

HENRY: Oh well, that's my hat-trick for the year, three title fights and three defeats. I thought I just nicked it tonight. I had him going in the fifth round but failed to finish it. Good luck to Joe. We're old pals and I wish him well. I'm not sure what I'm going to do now. I'll go away and have a good think, and talk things through with Jim and my brother George.

FIGHT NO. 21

- Venue: Westfalenhalle, Dortmund, 16 November 1957. Weight: 13st 7lb.
- Opponent: Hans Kalbfell (Germany). Weight: 14st 2lb.
- Result: WON points 10 rounds.

RINGSIDE REPORT (Johnny Sharpe, *Ring Magazine*): A rejuvenated Henry Cooper was carried around the ring in triumph in Dortmund by delighted German-based British soldiers after he had boxed majestically to outpoint Hans Kalbfell over ten rounds. Cooper's career looked on the rocks after four successive defeats, but the way he outclassed the highly rated German champion suggests he has been written off far too soon.

HENRY: That's as good as I've ever boxed. They brought me over here thinking I would be easy meat for Kalbfell, but they didn't know how hard I'd trained for this. I'm determined to get back on track after those three title-fight defeats.

FIGHT NO. 22

- Venue: Westfalenhalle, Dortmund, 11 January 1958. Weight: 13st 9lb.
- Opponent: Heinz Neuhaus (Germany). Weight: 15st 1lb.
- Result: DRAW 10 rounds.

RINGSIDE REPORT (Gilbert Odd, *Sporting Review*): Even the German fans booed the puzzling decision to give a draw at the end of ten rounds, at least seven of which were decisively won by a confident and composed Henry Cooper. Neuhaus laboured against Cooper's solid left jabs that were rarely out of his face as he tried to bully his way forward in predictable lines. They are talking of Neuhaus making a world title challenge, but on the evidence of this contest Cooper is much better suited for that elevated level of boxing.

HENRY: What a joke! As I went out for the tenth round Jim Wicks said, 'You've just got to stay on your feet to win.' It's the first draw I've ever had, but I know in my heart that I won by a mile. Still, it's better than a defeat.

FIGHT NO. 23

- Venue: Festhalle, Frankfurt, 19 April 1958. Weight: 13st 5lb.
- Opponent: Erich Schoeppner (Germany). Weight: 12st 8lb.
- Result: LOST, disqualified round 6.

RINGSIDE REPORT (Alan Hoby, *Sunday Express*): Henry Cooper was robbed here in Frankfurt after throwing a perfect punch that knocked German light-heavyweight champion Erich Schoeppner cold in the sixth round of their scheduled ten rounder. The Bellingham Belter had no sooner had his hand raised in victory than the German boxing officials decided instead to disqualify him for an alleged and illegal rabbit punch. Henry's mighty left hook landed on Schoeppner's ear as he turned to try to avoid it. No way was it a foul blow. The only person who does not know of the scandalously reversed decision is Schoeppner. He is on his way to hospital, still unconscious.

HENRY: This is the first time I've ever been disqualified as a pro. It's diabolical. My punch was aimed at the jaw, but he turned and took it on the ear. I've never rabbit punched anybody in my life. The referee didn't say a dickie bird, but German officials cooked up the change of decision among themselves.

FIGHT NO. 24

- Venue: Coney Beach, Porthcawl, 3 September 1958. Weight: 13st 4lb.
- Opponent: Dick Richardson (Newport). Weight: 14st 9lb.
- Result: WON, knockout round 5.

RINGSIDE REPORT (Steve Fagan, *Daily Sketch*): Henry Cooper got off the canvas here at Porthcawl to knockout Dick Richardson with a left hook that lifted the giant Welshman off the ground before he fell backwards, out to the world. It was a fifth round punch that could be measured on the Richter scale, and confirmed that the Bellingham twin is back in business as a championship contender.

HENRY: When I went down in the fifth, Dick made the mistake of thinking I was in trouble, when all I was doing was gathering my senses. He was a wide-open target as he came rushing at me. I have rarely hit anybody harder than that, and the moment I connected, I knew it was 'Goodnight, Dick'.

FIGHT NO. 25

- Venue: Wembley Pool, 14 October 1958. Weight: 13st 5lb.
- Opponent: Zora Folley (USA). Weight: 14st 2lb
- Result: WON points, 10 rounds.

RINGSIDE REPORT (Reg Gutteridge, London *Evening News*): What a difference a year makes! This time last year Henry Cooper looked washed up after four defeats on the trot. Now he is buoyant as a genuine world title contender after this stunning ten rounds points victory over number three challenger Zora Folley. Cooper had some uncomfortable moments, including a brief visit to the canvas in round three, but his efficient jabbing and ringcraft gave him a distinct edge over his illustrious opponent, who many considered the best heavyweight on the planet.

HENRY: He caught me with a good right hand early on, but it was a wake-up call and I made sure I wasn't around when he kept trying to repeat the punch. I kept whacking him with counter punches as he set himself to throw the right, and I was finding him easy to hit as he tired in the second half of the fight.

'Zora Folley ducks Henry's lead and lands with a body shot'

FIGHT NO. 26

- Venue: Earls Court, 12 January 1959. Weight: 13st 8lb.
- Opponent: Brian London (Blackpool). Weight: 14st 12lb.
- Result: WON points, 15 rounds (British and Empire heavyweight title).

RINGSIDE REPORT (Jack Wilson, *Boxing News*): Tamed, tormented and tantalised by a superb left hand boxing display by Henry Cooper, Britain's heavyweight Lion, Brian London, went out like a lamb in his first British and Empire title defence. Both boxers bled profusely as Cooper won by the length of Blackpool Promenade and gave the outgoing champion the boxing lesson of his life. An indication of just how bemused and bruised London was is that he held up Cooper's arm in victory at the end of the fourteenth round. It must have come as an unpleasant shock to discover there were still three more minutes of misery to come!

HENRY: We had the needle before the fight because of the silly things Brian was saying. He was obviously trying to get under my skin but it didn't work. In fact, it just made me more determined to beat him good and proper, just to shut him up. But he was very sporting in defeat and now we can be pals and put the past behind us. It was nice of him to hold up my hand as the winner with a round still to go. Jim Wicks called it a 'half-time score', but it was more like injury-time.

FIGHT NO. 27

- Venue: Coney Beach, Porthcawl, 26 August 1959. Weight: 13st 3lb.
- Opponent: Gawie de Klerk (South Africa). Weight: 13st 11lb.
- Result: WON referee stopped fight round 5 (British Empire heavyweight title).

RINGSIDE REPORT (Gerard Walter, *News Chronicle*): It took four rounds for Henry Cooper to shake off his ring rust, then he went to work on his South African challenger Gawie de Klerk and finished him off in the fifth round of this British Empire title fight. The contest was scheduled for fifteen rounds, but as soon as Cooper applied real pressure, de Klerk folded under a battery of left hooks. He visited the canvas twice and did not know whether he was in Porthcawl or Pretoria before the referee came to his rescue as Cooper hammered him against the ropes.

HENRY: It took me time to find my rhythm and I knew I needed to be careful after he'd clumped me with a big right hand in the opening round. Once I got my range I knew I could take him out because his defence was not the best. Now I want to be more active. I don't like having long lay-offs between fights, but Jim says we're not fighting for the taxman, who takes a huge bite out of every purse.

FIGHT NO. 28

- Venue: Wembley Pool, 17 November 1959. Weight: 13st 6lb.
- Opponent: Joe Erskine (Cardiff). Weight: 13st 10lb.
- Result: WON referee stopped fight round 12 (British and Empire heavyweight titles).

RINGSIDE REPORT (Tim Riley, *Boxing News*): In one of the most stunning and spectacular finishes ever to a British heavyweight title fight, Henry Cooper left his old rival Joe Erskine spread across the bottom rope in the twelfth round like a giant bow over a violin string. The Welsh warrior had just taken two counts and the referee was thinking of jumping in when Cooper landed with a ferocious left hook that sent Erskine backwards and through the ropes. He went out like a light and there was no need for a count. It was imperative to shift him off the bottom rope, and fears that he might have broken his back were, thank goodness, unfounded.

HENRY: We were worried that we'd badly hurt Joe, but I've been in the dressing-room to see him and he's fine. I've never seen a boxer go through the ropes like that that before. This is a tough old game, but once the punching is over we're always pals. Joe and I go back a long way to our Army days together and he's a smashing bloke.

Our fights are usually close, but tonight I always had the measure of him. His manager Benny Jacobs is kicking up a stink because I landed with a punch as the bell rang to end the fifth. It was on its way before the bell rang. Joe knows I would never deliberately foul him.

FIGHT NO. 29

- Venue: Wembley Pool, 13 September 1960. Weight: 13st 2lb.
- Opponent: Roy Harris (USA). Weight: 13st 1lb.
- Result: WON points 10 rounds.

RINGSIDE REPORT (Freddie Deards, *Reynolds News*): Recently married Henry Cooper husbanded his energy against Texan Roy Harris, and was a clear points winner over ten interesting rather than exciting rounds. Unusually for an American, Harris fought mainly on the retreat, which meant Cooper could not make an impact with his preferred counter punches because he was too busy forcing the pace. Harris took Floyd Patterson twelve rounds in a world title challenge, so we now know that Cooper is comfortable in world-class company.

HENRY: Harris had done his homework and knew all about my left hook. He continually moved to his left to nullify it. I felt very rusty in the early rounds, but I was never in any trouble and was always boxing within myself. There wouldn't have been a fight if I hadn't gone after him – he was only interested in boxing in reverse gear.

FIGHT NO. 30

- Venue: Wembley Pool, 12 December 1960. Weight: 13st 1lb.
- Opponent: Alex Miteff (Argentina). Weight: 15st 1lb.
- Result: WON points 10 rounds.

RINGSIDE REPORT (Charlie Hull, *Exchange Telegraph*): Strolling to a comfortable ten rounds points victory, Henry Cooper got careless against Argentina's bull-strong Alex Miteff and walked into a swinging right that dropped him for a nine count in the final round. The British champion survived a final flurry by Miteff to emerge a clear but rattled winner.

HENRY: Jim has given my earhole a bashing for that silly moment in the last round. It was the only time in the fight that he landed anything like a telling punch, and it caught me off balance. It just goes to show that in this game there's always danger around the corner. But on the whole I'm pleased with my performance. Miteff is no mug and has beaten the likes of Nino Valdes and Alonzo Johnson, and apart from that stupid knockdown, I was always his guvnor.

FIGHT NO. 31

- Venue: Wembley Pool, 21 March 1961. Weight: 13st 5lb.
- Opponent: Joe Erskine (Cardiff). Weight: 13st 12lb.
- Result: WON referee stopped fight 5 rounds (British and Empire title).

RINGSIDE REPORT (Steve Fagan, *Daily Sketch*): For fifteen minutes of legalised mayhem, Henry Cooper stabbed his left hand into the face of his old rival Joe Erskine until his face was a mask of blood. It was a relief to spectators in general and old Joe in particular when the referee waved this British and Empire title fight over at the end of the fifth round with Erskine hardly able to see through two swollen and cut eyes. The victory gives Cooper a coveted Lonsdale Belt outright.

HENRY: That was the easiest win I've had over Joe in all our fights. We just couldn't miss him with the left jab and I would not let Joe get into that rhythm of his when he is one of the world's classiest boxers. I'm thrilled to be taking home the Lonsdale Belt as my own property. It's one of the greatest prizes in sport.

FIGHT NO. 32

- Venue: Wembley Pool, 5 December 1961. Weight: 13st 2lb.
- Opponent: Zora Folley (USA). Weight: 13st 7lb.
- Result: LOST, knocked out round 2.

RINGSIDE REPORT (Reg Gutteridge, London *Evening News*): Plans for Henry Cooper to challenge Floyd Patterson for the world heavyweight crown went out of the window with this shock knockout defeat by Zora Folley. The second round punch that did the damage – a short, shuddering right to the jaw – sent Cooper into slumberland and he would not have beaten two counts. It is a big backward step for the Bellingham Bomber, who was a convincing points winner over world-ranked Folley when they last met three years ago. Henry failed to climb the same mountain twice.

HENRY: It's a fact that I've been having specialist treatment on my left elbow and it interrupted my training, but I can't use that as an excuse for this defeat. Folley is a class fighter and caught me with a cracking punch. It was a case of 'Goodnight nurse'. For the first time I trained at home for this fight, and Jim says it will be the last time. He says I've become soft, but regardless that punch would have taken anybody out.

FIGHT NO. 33

- Venue: Wembley Pool, 23 January 1962. Weight: 13st 3lb.
- Opponent: Tony Hughes (USA). Weight: 13st 9lb.
- Result: WON referee stopped fight 5 rounds.

RINGSIDE REPORT (Bill Martin, *Press Association*): Rocky Marciano's protégé Tony Hughes showed none of his mentor's aggression before being unhinged by Henry Cooper's lethal left hook. The punch to the jaw, delivered in the fifth round, had Hughes out on his feet and the referee was right to step in as the British champion prepared to follow up with even heavier ammunition.

HENRY: Rocky was one of my idols and it was a bit daunting to know he was in the opposite corner, but thank goodness only as a second! It's good to get back into a winning groove and this win has done my confidence a lot of good.

FIGHT NO. 34

- Venue: Belle Vue, Manchester, 26 February 1962. Weight: 13st 7lb.
- Opponent: Wayne Bethea (USA). Weight: 15st 8lb.
- Result: WON points 10 rounds.

RINGSIDE REPORT (Frank McGhee, *Daily Mirror*): New York-based Wayne Bethea arrived with a good reputation, including such impressive scalps as old Ezzard Charles and young Ernie Terrell, but he found Henry Cooper far too smart and ring-wise. Winning comfortably on points, Cooper tamed the American with his always-accurate left jab and often had him seeking the safety of a clinch after clubbing him with his trusted left hook.

HENRY: He was a cagey old pro and every time I thought I had him going, he would grab me and lock me in a clinch. The only danger to me was that he might strangle or crush me! He was a big old lump and felt like a sack of coal when he leaned on me. My confidence is back after that nightmare against Folley.

FIGHT NO. 35

- Venue: Nottingham Ice Rink, 2 April 1962. Weight: 13st 7lb.
- Opponent: Joe Erskine (Cardiff). Weight: 14st 2lb.
- Result: WON referee stopped fight 9 rounds (British and Empire titles).

RINGSIDE REPORT (Desmond Hackett, *Daily Express*): Henry Cooper has just about won Joe Erskine outright now and should be entitled to take him home and put him on his mantel shelf. This was their eighth meeting including their amateur contests, and the Englishman leads the Welshman 5–3, including three successive victories in which Erskine has been strictly second best. Cooper's left jab was in Erskine's face like an angry wasp throughout the fight and old Joe's features were a bloody mess when the referee rescued him from the torture chamber after nine painfully one-sided rounds.

HENRY: I think me and Joe have had enough of hitting each other now. Our contests used to be even-steven, but in the last three fights, he has hardly been in it. I wish him luck with his future, but I don't think it will include any more fights with me. I'm sick of the sight of him in the ring, but will be happy to meet him anytime outside as a pal.

'Joe Erskine rolls on the ropes under Henry's two-fisted assault'

FIGHT NO. 36

- Venue: Wembley Pool, 26 March 1963. Weight: 13st 6lb.
- Opponent: Dick Richardson (Newport). Weight: 14st 9lb.
- Result: WON stopped fight 5 rounds (British and Empire titles).

RINGSIDE REPORT (Peter Lorenzo, *Daily Herald*): For the first time that anybody could remember, Gentleman Henry Cooper lost his temper in the ring after Dick Richardson had hit him after the bell at the end of the third round. The two fighters had to be pulled apart as they went for each other like angry bulls. The Welshman was made to pay for his overtime punch when Cooper flattened him with a series of rapid left hooks in the fifth round. The referee waved it over as the Newport giant struggled to get off the canvas. This was a repeat of Cooper's victory at Porthcawl five years ago, and the whisper is it could have set up a showdown with the Louisville Lip, Cassius Clay.

HENRY: Dick can be a bully if you let him get away with things, so when he hit me after the bell I hit him back so that he knew he couldn't take liberties. Jim has given me a telling off, but I would do the same thing again if anybody tries any foul stuff: you have to fight fire with fire.

FIGHT NO. 37

- Venue: Wembley Stadium, 18 June 1963. Weight: 13st 3lb. (Henry actually weighed 12st 12lb, but Jim Wicks placed lead weights in his boots.)
- Opponent: Cassius Clay (USA). Weight: 14st 9lb.
- Result: LOST referee stopped fight 5 rounds (cut eye).

RINGSIDE REPORT (Frank Butler, *News of the World*): Gaseous Cassius Clay did exactly as he prophesied when he stopped Henry Cooper in the fifth round at Wembley Stadium, but Our Enery very nearly shut his big mouth and came oh so close to one of the upsets of the century. Enery's 'Ammer – one of the most vicious left hooks in the business – floored Clay in the closing seconds of the fourth round. No winning goal at Wembley has brought a bigger roar as the arrogant American crashed back into the ropes and onto the seat of his pants. He was in a complete fog of despair as the bell came to his rescue with the count at four. He wobbled back to the refuge of his corner on rubber legs that were betraying him with every step, and his wily trainer Angelo Dundee won him extra precious recovery seconds by complaining about a torn glove. Clay the clown came out for the fifth round with serious intent, and hit Cooper with a stream of deadly left jabs that worsened a cut over the British champion's eye to the point where the referee had no option but to call it off as blood gushed from the wound. I wonder what story I might have been writing had Henry landed his pet punch just ten seconds earlier?

'Henry prepares to throw the 'Ammer that floored Clay'

HENRY: If only I'd had another minute, I reckon I could have finished him off. Anybody who has watched me over the years knows

I never let anybody off the hook if I've got them going and Clay was in a right state when he got up. But what can you do? The old mince pie let me down and we couldn't argue when the ref stopped it. At least we shut him up for a while. To be honest, I quite like the bloke and all that shouting before the fight got bums on seats. So we can't complain. At least I think I've won his respect. Didn't do bad for a bum and a cripple, did I?

FIGHT NO. 38

- Venue: Belle Vue, Manchester, 24 February 1964. Weight: 13st 6lb.
- Opponent: Brian London (Blackpool). Weight: 14st 11lb.
- Result: WON points 15 rounds (British, Empire & vacant European titles).

RINGSIDE REPORT (Sydney Hulls, *Daily Express*): Henry Cooper added the European crown to his title collection and won a second Lonsdale Belt outright after comfortably outpointing Brian London over fifteen one-sided rounds. This is the third time that Cooper has grounded the Blackpool Bomber, who was gracious to admit afterwards that Henry has now won him outright. As champion of Europe, Cooper has first claim on a world title challenge once Liston and Clay have sorted out their differences.

HENRY: Brian and I used to be sworn enemies, but we have got to like each other and he was sporting enough to concede that I'm his guvnor. I couldn't miss him with my left jab and he took his punishment like a man. Now we'll watch the Liston/Ali situation with close interest.

FIGHT NO. 39

- Venue: Royal Albert Hall, 16 November 1964. Weight: 13st 6lb.
- Opponent: Roger Rischer (USA). Weight: 14st 2lb.
- Result: LOST points 10 rounds

RINGSIDE REPORT (Reg Gutteridge, London *Evening News*): It's not often that Britain's favourite boxer Henry Cooper hears boos, but the jeers from the Albert Hall crowd were shared equally between both the British champion and his mauling, spoiling opponent Roger Rischer after a boring ten round battle narrowly won by the American. It could have passed as a wrestling rather than boxing match, with the referee continually trying to pull the two rivals apart. It was not a pretty sight.

HENRY: Hands up, probably my worst performance as a professional, but it takes two to tango and Rischer just didn't want to fight. He grabbed me at every opportunity and we finished up with a real stinkeroo. It was a clash of styles, and only one of us came to fight. The quicker we forget it, the better.

FIGHT NO. 40

- Venue: Royal Albert Hall, 12 January 1965. Weight: 13st 7lb.
- Opponent: Dick Wipperman (USA). Weight: 14st 7lb.
- Result: WON referee stopped fight 5 rounds.

RINGSIDE REPORT (Donald Saunders, *Daily Telegraph*): Dick Wipperman, billed as 'The wild buffalo from Buffalo', was cut down to size by the left hooks of Henry Cooper after four even rounds in which both men concentrated on left jabs from distance. A change of tactics by Cooper in the fifth brought the British champion quick results, and the tall American suddenly wilted as he took a series of hooks to the jaw that had him sending out distress signals, bringing a merciful intervention by the referee.

HENRY: He had such a long left lead that I had problems getting close enough to land the hook, so I jabbed with him but was getting him into a frame of mind where he thought all I had was the jab. The moment I started bringing my punches in on an arc he was bang in bother. At least I got that Rischer result out of my system.

FIGHT NO. 41

- Venue: Wolverhampton Civic Hall, 20 April 1965. Weight: 13st 11lb.
- Opponent: Chip Johnson (USA). Weight: 13st 7lb.
- Result: WON knockout round 1.

RINGSIDE REPORT (Steve Fagan, *Daily Sketch*): Oh brother, what a night of revenge for the Coopers! Five months ago Chip Johnson virtually ended Jim Cooper's career when he cut him so badly he was forced to announce his retirement. Last night identical twin Henry made Johnson pay with an incredible first round knockout victory, his famed and feared left hook landing with such venom that the American was out before he had hit the canvas.

HENRY: That was for George. I've never been more determined to beat an opponent. Johnson got his comeuppance for saying stupid things before the fight, like what he'd done to one brother he could do to the other. That'll teach him to keep his mouth shut. Everybody's trying to be an Ali these days. More rabbit than Sainsbury's!

FIGHT NO. 42

- Venue: St Andrew's Stadium, Birmingham, 15 June 1965. Weight: 13st 4lb.
- Opponent: Johnny Prescott (Birmingham) Weight: 13st 9lb.
- Result: WON retired round 10 (British and Empire titles).

RINGSIDE REPORT (Frank McGhee, *Daily Mirror*): Johnny Prescott, the Boxing Beau Brummel of Birmingham, put up a brave show against Henry Cooper, but manager George Biddles did him a favour by pulling him out of this British and Empire title fight after taking steady punishment for ten frantic rounds. The biggest danger to Cooper was being drowned during rain storms that swept over the Birmingham City football ground. Heavy body punches knocked the fight out of Prescott and he took two counts in the tenth round before Biddles decided his man had nothing left to give.

HENRY: Johnny is a good, strong boy but I knew he was struggling when I started digging punches into his body. I could hear him grunting, and so I abandoned my jabbing and kept up the attack downstairs. It was wise to retire him because he knew I was completely in charge.

FIGHT NO. 43

- Venue: Wembley Pool, 19 October 1965. Weight: 13st 8lb.
- Opponent: Amos Johnson (USA). Weight: 14st.
- Result: LOST points 10 rounds.

RINGSIDE REPORT (Jack Wood, *Daily Mail*): There are whispers of a world title fight for Henry Cooper, but he may have wrecked the script by dropping a points decision to the ambling Amos Johnson. When Henry has an off night it is not a pretty sight, and he struggled to get his usual rhythm against an awkward but well-schooled opponent. Even so, I had Cooper winning by a round, and the crowd booed the decision. It was a nightmare for Cooper from the moment in the first round when a punch well below the border dropped him, but the referee let the American off with a warning.

HENRY: I thought I did enough to win, but admit I boxed badly. It was one of those nights when I just couldn't find my range and that punch in the first round hit me right in the family jewellery and knocked me out of my stride. I'm aching in a place where you wouldn't show your mum. There's talk about me getting a title fight with Ali, but that's all it is at the moment, talk. I'll believe it when it happens. Didn't do myself any favours tonight, did I?

FIGHT NO. 44

- Venue: Olympia, London, 25 January 1966. Weight: 13st 10lb.
- Opponent: Hubert Hilton (USA) Weight: 14st.
- Result: WON referee stopped fight round 2.

RINGSIDE REPORT (Donald Saunders, *Daily Telegraph*): This fight was staged in the circus ring at Olympia but British champion Henry Cooper was in no mood for clowning as he dispatched the tall, dark and hazardous Hubert Hilton in two rounds. Ranked ninth in the world, Hilton promised all sorts of evil intent before the fight, but was wrecked by a devastating left hook that instantaneously knocked the fight out of him and brought the referee's intervention as he fell flat to the canvas.

HENRY: I know a world title fight could be around the corner, so I dare not slip up again. I wanted to get Hilton out of there as quickly as possible because he's a dangerous guy if you let him get on top. He knocked out Bodell and Prescott, but that put me on alert and I made sure I got in first.

FIGHT NO. 45

- Venue: Wolverhampton Civic Hall, 16 February 1966. Weight: 13st 8lb.
- Opponent: Jefferson Davis (USA). Weight: 14st 3lb.
- Result: WON knockout round 1.

RINGSIDE REPORT (Sydney Hulls, *Daily Express*): Jefferson Davis came, saw and was conquered in just 100 seconds, the quickest win of Henry Cooper's career. It was another revenge win for the Cooper twins, and Davis never looked like repeating the victory he had enjoyed against Jim Cooper three years ago. Henry landed his 'Ammer with such force that the count was a mere formality. Muhammad Ali, haunted by memories of Wembley, will have made careful note of the finishing punch as he prepares to put his world title on the line against Cooper.

HENRY: It's no secret that Jim is negotiating a world title fight for me. That's been my dream since I first pulled on boxing gloves. I like it here at the Civic Hall. Two fights, two first round wins!

FIGHT NO. 46

- Venue: Highbury Stadium, Arsenal, 21 May 1966. Weight: 13st 5lb.
- Opponent: Muhammad Ali (USA). Weight: 14st 3lb.
- Result: LOST referee stopped fight round 6 (cut eye) (World heavyweight title).

RINGSIDE REPORT (George Whiting, London *Evening Standard*): Henry (London Pride) Cooper, a craftsman seeking improbable dominion over an artist, gave of his best and gave of his blood until, after ninety-eight seconds of round six, a jagged, monstrous gash over his left eyebrow brought referee George Smith flinging wide his arms to signal that the war was over. There will forever be controversy about the exact manner of the bloodshot finish – Cooper claiming a butt, Clay insisting that the payoff came from the same downward right-hander that lowered Sonny Liston. The precise instant that the Cooper brow split asunder calls for sharper eyes than mine, but I would vote for a legitimate punch.

HENRY: I thought at first that Clay or Ali, or whatever he calls himself caught me with his head, but now I've had a chance to see film of the fight I accept that it was a punch that did the damage. We've now fought for eleven rounds and I think you'll find I'm ahead on points! Ali calls himself The Greatest. I'm not arguing. He's certainly the fastest. The ring was like a ballroom and I could not pin him with my left hook, like in our first fight because he was dancing away like Fred Astaire on roller skates.

FIGHT NO. 47

- Venue: Wembley Pool, 20 September 1966. Weight: 13st 8lb.
- Opponent: Floyd Patterson (USA). Weight: 13st 10lb.
- Result: LOST knockout round 4.

RINGSIDE REPORT (Desmond Hackett, *Daily Express*): They say the last thing a great champion loses is his punch. Floyd Patterson may be past his peak, but his punching power was there for all to see at Wembley.

The only person who did NOT see it is British folk hero Henry Cooper, who was knocked sparko by a right out of the blue midway through the fourth round. Recovering from a knockdown moments earlier, Cooper was a sitting duck for the punch that landed with such force that it turned him around before he fell face first to the canvas.

HENRY: You'll have to tell me what happened. I've no idea. One minute I was defending myself after being knocked down by the quickest punches I've ever faced, and the next Jim Wicks was asking if I was all right and I was down on the canvas. Floyd has been in to make sure I'm all right. He is not only a great fighter but also a real gentleman.

FIGHT NO. 48

- Venue: De Montfort Hall, Leicester, 17 April 1967. Weight: 13st 12lb.
- Opponent: Boston Jacobs (USA). Weight: 13st 9lb.
- Result: WON points 10 rounds.

RINGSIDE REPORT (Reg Gutteridge, London *Evening News*): Henry Cooper returned to the business of winning after his back-to-back defeats by world greats Muhammad Ali and Floyd Patterson, but against an opponent – Boston Jacobs – who is not even a household name in his own house. Cooper took time to shake off ring rust, but once he had settled into his stride won on points at a canter. Jacobs was a spoiling opponent who came to survive, and at the final bell at least had the satisfaction of still being on his feet. He will go home to the States with Henry Cooper's left fist tattooed on his face.

HENRY: I needed that to get my rhythm back. It was a good workout against an opponent who was more interested in stopping me hitting him than throwing any punches. Now we're going to look for some title defences.

FIGHT NO. 49

- Venue: Molineux, Wolverhampton, 13 June 1967. Weight: 13st 6lb.
- Opponent: Jack Bodell (Swadlincote). Weight: 14st 2lb.
- Result: WON referee stopped fight 2 rounds (British & Empire titles).

RINGSIDE REPORT (Steve Fagan, *Daily Sketch*): Manager George Biddles talked a good fight for his man Jack Bodell before this British and Empire title fight, but the Swadlincote chicken farmer could not put action to go with his words. Henry Cooper took one round to weigh up the swinging southpaw from Swadlincote and then at the start of the second had him trapped on the ropes taking a procession of left hooks to the jaw. The referee pulled Cooper off as Bodell sank to the canvas like a holed ship going down at sea, completely bemused and badly bruised. Henry may not have ruled the world, but he is without question king of his own back yard.

HENRY: It may have looked as if I was under pressure in that first round, but I was being calculating and wanted to lead Jack into a false sense of security. Our plan was not to open up with the big punches until we'd had a look at him. It worked to perfection.

FIGHT NO. 50

- Venue: Wembley Pool, 7 November 1967. Weight: 13st 4lb.
- Opponent: Billy Walker (West Ham). Weight: 13st 9lb.
- Result: WON referee stopped fight 6 rounds (British & Empire titles).

RINGSIDE REPORT (John Rodda, *The Guardian*): South Londoner Henry Cooper won a record third Lonsdale Belt outright at Wembley, but it was the East London idol Billy Walker who took the real belting. How ironic that Cooper – who can bleed for Britain – eventually won on cuts, Walker being sent back to his corner a third of the way through the sixth round with his face a crimson mask. The 'Battle of London' was settled by Cooper's powerful left jab, and I counted twenty punches crashing into Walker's face without response in what proved to be the final round. Walker should now urgently consider his future. It cannot be good for his health to use his face as an archery target.

'Henry's left jab crashes through Billy Walker's defence'

HENRY: I'm so proud to have won a third Lonsdale Belt outright. I will put them away in a vault and one day pass them on to my sons so they know their old Dad could fight a bit. Billy was brave, but he leads with his face too much. I couldn't miss him with the jab. Makes a change for my opponent to suffer the cuts instead of me. I like Billy a lot, and hope his injuries heal quickly.

FIGHT NO. 51

- Venue: Wembley Pool, 18 September 1968. Weight: 13st 3lb.
- Opponent: Karl Mildenberger (Germany). Weight: 14st 9lb.
- Result: WON disqualified round 8 (European title).

RINGSIDE REPORT (Donald Saunders, *Daily Telegraph*): Henry Cooper regained the European heavyweight title at Wembley when German southpaw Karl Mildenberger was disqualified in the eighth round for using his head as a third glove. There was an element of desperation about Mildenberger's work throughout the contest as Cooper's left jab and whiplash left hooks slowly broke him up, and he was close to a knockout defeat in the seventh round when sent sagging to the canvas for an eight count. His one weapon appeared to be wild use of his head, and he was warned several times before the Italian referee decided to disqualify him after Cooper had come out of a clinch with blood running down his battle-scarred face.

HENRY: That's the record put straight, because I never lost the European title in the ring and Mildenberger got it because an injury prevented me defending it. He played the part of the gentleman before and after the fight, but he was definitely trying to get the old nut in as he realised he was outgunned. I thought I did a good job on him.

FIGHT NO. 52

- Venue: Palazzetto dello Sport, Rome, 13 March 1969. Weight: 13st 5lb.
- Opponent: Piero Tomasoni (Italy). Weight: 13st 4lb.
- Result: WON knockout 5 rounds (European title).

RINGSIDE REPORT (Neil Allen, *The Times*): One of the roughest European title fights of all time ended with Henry Cooper hammering Italian challenger Piero Tomasoni to the canvas in the fifth round. As the ten-second count was tolled, the ring canvas became carpeted with rotten fruit and vegetables hurled by angry Italian fans. Tomasoni was like a wild bull after being dropped by a Cooper left hook in the first round, and attacked the champion with everything but the ringside stool. Amazingly the Dutch referee ignored the fact that many of his punches were landing below the belt and Cooper fell to his knees in agony, taking a nine count. It was another four rough and tumble rounds before Cooper finally tamed Tomasoni with what has famously become known as Enery's 'Ammer. The European champion later showed me his protective cup to prove that Tomasoni's punches had been so low that they had made a normally convex piece of sports equipment concave.

HENRY: That's the wildest fight I've ever been involved in. I couldn't believe what the referee was letting him get away with. I've got bruised thighs from where some of his punches landed, and his head was hardly out of my face. We thought we were going to get lynched when the referee counted Tomasoni out, but the fans switched to our side at the end and applauded us. Maybe it's because I've got an Italian wife?

FIGHT NO. 53

- Venue: Wembley Pool, 24 March 1970. Weight: 13st 13lb.
- Opponent: Jack Bodell (Swadlincote). Weight: 14st 10lb.
- Result: WON points 15 rounds (British & Empire titles).

RINGSIDE REPORT (Colin Hart, *The Sun*): Henry Cooper had to go fifteen bruising rounds with the always awkward Jack Bodell before he regained the British and Empire titles that he gave up in disgust when the Board of Control stopped him fighting Jimmy Ellis for a version of the world championship. Our Enery was always the guvnor against the Swadlincote southpaw, but had his feet trodden on so many times by the clumsy Bodell that he needed a chiropodist rather than Jim Wicks in his corner. Cooper won by the length of the Old Kent Road and had the Derbyshire man down three times, but at least Bodell improved on his two-round destruction of 1967.

HENRY: If there were prizes for being awkward, Jack would be a world champion. I've got bruised feet and shins where he kept stamping on me. He doesn't mean it; he's just born clumsy. That's two titles back. Our target now is to regain the European championship that they took away because of my injuries.

FIGHT NO. 54

- Venue: Wembley Pool, 10 November 1970. Weight: 13st 7lb.
- Opponent: Jose Urtain (Spain). Weight: 13st 11lb.
- Result: WON referee stopped fight round 8 (European title).
-

RINGSIDE REPORT (Reg Gutteridge, London *Evening News*): Jose Urtain got his mighty physique from lifting rocks in his Spanish homeland, and at Wembley he must have felt as if the Rock of Gibraltar had fallen on him after Henry Cooper had finished bashing him up. Britain's most popular sportsman regained the European crown with a commanding performance, jabbing the defending champion into dizzy disarray until the referee intervened to say 'No way Jose' and led him back to his corner bloodied and beaten after eight demanding rounds. Yes, it was the final curtain for Urtain.

HENRY: It just shows you that being strong doesn't necessarily make you a good fighter. His boxing technique was all over the place and I found him dead easy to hit with my jabs. I'm sure if it was a weightlifting competition I would come second best to him, but boxing is about more than muscle. Anyway, we're delighted to have all our three titles back.

FIGHT NO. 55

- Venue: Wembley Pool, 16 March 1971. Weight: 13st 5lb.
- Opponent: Joe Bugner (Bedford). Weight: 15st 2lb.
- Result: LOST points 15 rounds (British, European & Empire titles).

RINGSIDE REPORT (Peter Wilson, *Daily Mirror*): Harry Gibbs is one of the finest referees I have seen in more than forty years of reporting boxing, but last night in my view he got it badly wrong when he adjudged Joe Bugner the fifteen rounds points winner over Henry Cooper in a dramatic triple title fight. On a decibel count, it was clear that most of the booing and jeering capacity Wembley crowd agreed with my reading of the fight. I made Cooper a clear winner by two points, and I just cannot understand how Gibbs managed to see the 21-year-old Bugner the master of the 37-year-old icon of British heavyweight boxing. After the disappointment of his defeat, Our Enery announced he would be hanging up his gloves. What a sad way for it all to end. One of my favourite sporting personalities deserved to go out a winner, and the way I saw the fight that is exactly what he did do, but it is the impressively built but robotic Bugner who walks off with Henry's titles. There's no justice.

HENRY: That's it, gentlemen. That's me lot.

BREAKDOWN:

- 55 fights (374 rounds, 18 hours 7 minutes of ring action).
- 44 opponents (Joe Erskine five times, Brian London three times, Uber Bacilieri, Joe Bygraves, Zora Folley, Dick Richardson, Jack Bodell and Muhammad Ali twice).
- 40 victories (27 inside the distance, 11 on points, 2 disqualifications).
- 14 defeats (8 inside the distance, 5 on points, 1 disqualification).
- 1 draw.
- Henry conceded weight in all but 8 of his 55 fights.
- 1 May 2011, the final bell rang for Henry Cooper two days before his seventy-seventh birthday.
- He will be remembered always as a champion human being and a Hero for All Time.

That's it. That's me lot.

Also by Norman Giller

Banks of England (with Gordon Banks)
Football and All That: A History of the Beautiful Game
Know What I Mean (with Frank Bruno)
Eye of the Tiger (with Frank Bruno)
From Zero to Hero (with Frank Bruno)
My Most Memorable Fights (with Henry Cooper)
How to Box (with Henry Cooper)
Henry Cooper's 100 Greatest Boxers
Mike Tyson, the Release of Power (with Reg Gutteridge)
Let's Be Honest (with Reg Gutteridge)